When shall they rest?

When shall they rest?

THE CHEROKEES' LONG STRUGGLE WITH AMERICA

by Peter Collier

HOLT, RINEHART AND WINSTON
NEW YORK   CHICAGO   SAN FRANCISCO

In memory of my father, Donovan Collier, a good man who never forgot the days when he was a boy and Indians came to set up summer camp on his father's land.

A HOLT REINFORCED EDITION
Copyright © 1973 by Peter Collier
All rights reserved, including the right to reproduce
this book or portions thereof in any form.
Published simultaneously in Canada by
Holt, Rinehart and Winston of Canada, Limited
Printed in the United States of America
Designed by Kathleen F. Westray
Photo Research by Enid Klass
FIRST EDITION
Library of Congress Cataloging in Publication Data
Collier, Peter.
    When shall they rest?
    SUMMARY: A history of the Cherokees emphasizing
their continuous mistreatment by the white man
and the United States government.
    1. Cherokee Indians—Government relations—
Juvenile literature. [1. Cherokee Indians—
History. 2. Indians of North America—History]
I. Title.
E99.C5C68   970.5   73-6675
ISBN   0-03-091977-0

CONTENTS

ACKNOWLEDGMENTS

Acknowledgment is made to the following for permission to reproduce the photographs in this book:

to Mrs. Mildred P. Ballenger, for the photograph of a contemporary Cherokee home.

to the Library of Congress, for the photograph of Sequoyah.

to the Oklahoma Historical Society, for the photographs of "The Run," September 16, 1893; and Redbird Smith and friend.

to the Philbrook Art Center, Tulsa, Oklahoma, for the photographs of the paintings, *Cherokee Indian Ball Game* by Cecil Dick, and *Old Cherokee Chief's Home* by Paul Rogers; and for the photographs of the paintings of John Ross and Mrs. John Ross.

to the Smithsonian Institution, National Anthropological Archives, for the photographs of the Cherokee Indians brought to London and the Cherokee alphabet; and for the portraits of John Ridge and John Ross as a young man.

to UPI, for the photograph of William Wayne Keeler.

to the Western History Collections, University of Oklahoma Library, for the photographs of the Old Cherokee Capitol; the Cherokee National Female Seminary; the Cherokee National Female Seminary students; the Cherokee Male Seminary; the run of September 16, 1893, showing the first train leaving the line for Perry, Oklahoma; the 1889 run; The Ridge (Major Ridge); Stand Watie.

"Now, we shall not rest until we have regained our rightful place. We shall tell our young people what we know. We shall send them to the corners of the earth to learn more. They shall lead us.

"Now, we have much to do. When our task is done, we will be ready to rest.

"In these days, intruders, named without our consent, speak for the Cherokees. When the Cherokee government is the Cherokee people, we shall rest.

"In these days, the high courts of the United States listen to people who have been wronged. When our wrongs have been judged in these courts, and the illegalities of the past have been corrected, we shall rest.

"In these days, there are countless ways by which people make their grievances known to all Americans. When we have learned these new ways that bring strength and power, and we have used them, we shall rest.

"In these days, we are losing our homes and our children's homes. When our homeland is protected, for ourselves and for the generations to follow, we shall rest.

"In the vision of our creator, we declare ourselves ready to stand proudly among the nationalities of these United States."

—DECLARATION OF THE FIVE
COUNTY CHEROKEE MOVEMENT, 1966

PROLOGUE:
The Exiles

Back in the green rolling hills of northeastern Oklahoma, in a deserted clearing a stone's throw off a rough gravel road, there is a small family cemetery. Partly overgrown by bunch-grass and vines and bordered by a wooden stile fence covered with honeysuckle and wild lavender, it is silent except for the busy noise of bees and cicada. As the afternoon sun slants in through the dogwood trees, long shadows crawl over the gravestones. A few of these markers are small and bear only the first name of a child who didn't live long past his birth. Others are larger, the inscriptions chiselled into the smooth marble almost eaten away by time and weather. Slightly apart from the rest is the inconspicuous grave of a remarkable Indian leader, John Ross, Principal Chief of the Cherokee Nation from 1827 until his death in 1866.

This forty-year span was the golden age of the Cherokees. When the United States government dealt with them it dealt with a fiercely independent nation, not a conquered people. Back in their Georgia homeland, in the 1790s when John Ross was still a boy, these Indians had dropped the weapons that had once made them one of the most formidable tribes in the New World and picked up the plowshare offered by the white man. Almost overnight they exchanged their native dwellings for log cabins and became tillers of the field instead of hunters. They created a model republic with a bicameral legislature, an eloquent constitution, and a comprehensive judicial system. After a native genius named Sequoyah invented a Cherokee alphabet, the people attained almost total literacy. They established a national printing press, a newspaper, and the best schools in their part of the country.

But nothing could keep their fragile dream of living on equal terms with the whites from being shattered. In 1838 they were driven out of the land where their fathers were buried, and sent on a death march that would be engraved in tribal memory as the "Trail of Tears." One-quarter of the Cherokee Nation died along the way. Those who survived came here to Oklahoma, picked up the shards of their national life and began again. But despite the Cherokees' limitless good faith, they were forced to stand by helplessly as even their new lands were taken from them. In the end, the Cherokees understood the Cheyenne Dull Knife's bitter words about white men: "They made us many promises, more than I can remember, but they never kept but one; they promised to take our land, and they took it."

As you drive through this broad sweep of country today you see forests of television antennas standing over new housing tracts, long cars flashing down super highways, oil rigs pumping endlessly at the ground, and other signs of

2

modern America. But in the solitude of the Ross cemetery it is easy to let your imagination drift back to the time—less than a hundred years ago—when the newly arrived Cherokees were the only civilized people in this part of the Wild West. They were surrounded by white desperadoes fleeing the long arm of the law and by local tribes like the Osages, their faces painted in fierce colors and eagle feathers dancing from their roached hair. This area was not called Oklahoma then, but Indian Territory. Nearby Tahlequah was not a city of white merchants and college students as it is today, but the capital of an Indian republic known throughout the world.

The small family cemetery where John Ross rests is a mute witness to great accomplishments and to a time when Indians were not a hidden minority in the white man's land, but a proud and prosperous people in their own. But it is also a poignant reminder that the Cherokee Nation is no more and that whites now occupy what red men pioneered.

Oklahomans are not ashamed of their Indian past. In the thriving city of Tahlequah they point proudly to the landmarks left by this unique nation: the country administration building in the town square that began as the capitol of the Cherokees; the town jail that was constructed ninety years ago as their National Prison; the squat gray structure where the Indians' Supreme Court sat. Oklahomans readily admit that their own society is built on a bedrock of Cherokee culture and say they are grateful for the rich legacy the Indians left their state. (The very name Oklahoma comes from the language of the Choctaws, the Cherokees' neighbors, and means "red man.") Indeed, to be able to claim a fraction of Cherokee blood, name some distant relative who came over the Trail of Tears, or perhaps even produce a frayed, sepia-toned photograph of that square-jawed Indian face is to establish a pedigree as good for Oklahomans as that of the New England Brahmin who can pull out a family tree connecting him to the fretting Puritans.

But Indians are still fixed in the minds of white Oklahomans as part of the past. If they are important, it is only because they are an undeniable element in the complex chemistry of history that finally produced Oklahoma. Oklahomans insist that the Indians who once ruled here have been assimilated through intermarriage and otherwise accepted as equal partners in white society. Many of them were. But if you press them hard enough, the white people of Tahlequah finally shrug their shoulders and gesture vaguely toward the verdant hills and hollows surrounding the town. They will admit that there are still a few "old full bloods" living "out yonder," Indians who were not assimilated and who have stubbornly maintained their old ways. But whites make it clear that in their way of thinking to be such a Cherokee today is to be a museum piece.

This view of the Indian is a myth. The Cherokee full bloods did not simply drift into the mainstream of America when their lands became part of the new state of Oklahoma. More than ten thousand of them still live today in full-blood settlements throughout the Oklahoma Ozarks. They speak little English and live according to the ideals of harmony and community that have survived from olden times. They are invisible men. Early on in their dealings with the American, the Cherokees adopted his style of dress and many of his outward habits, and they do not draw attention to themselves today by performing quaint rituals in feathered headdresses before the clicking cameras of tourists. There is nothing in their lifestyle to force them into the field of vision of those who would like to believe they have disappeared.

How did the descendants of a great and powerful Nation

wind up living in grinding poverty in dilapidated mountain cabins? How did the millions of acres they once owned get into the hands of the white man? How did they become trapped in a social system that says they don't exist at the same time it continues to take the little they have managed to hang onto from better days?

The story of the Cherokees, from the first New World contact with the whites until the present time, is the story of a people who couldn't escape, no matter how hard or ingeniously they tried. Their resistance was not as stirring as that of the Sioux and Cheyenne, who whipped up their ponies for a last desperate stand against the American soldiers who swept murderously through their country. Under the leadership of men like John Ross, the Cherokees followed a different course. They took the Great Father at his word and accepted his suggestion that they adopt the arts of white civilization. Long before the U.S. Cavalry rode into the middle of America on its mission of death, the Cherokees had adopted enough of white culture to be the envy of the rough-and-ready frontiersmen living all around them. But this too was resistance, their way of protecting their life and liberty, and in the end the consequences the Cherokees faced were no less tragic than the long death of the Plains tribes.

The fate of the Cherokees, more than that of any other tribe, shows the depth of the white man's malice. For even a tribe that could not be called "murdering redskins" faced annihilation; a nation that chose to protect itself by arguing constitutional issues with wit and daring in the marbled halls of Congress was treated the same as those that killed settlers and burned the wagon trains spreading over their country. The Cherokees were pushed until they had nowhere else to go and robbed until they had nothing more to take. Finally they became a nation in exile.

The cemetery where John Ross lies should be a national monument, but instead is obscure and forgotten. The Cherokees, too, are ignored even though they still exist inside white history, as they have for two centuries, like Jonah in the belly of the whale. Their story is an American epic, rarely told because it is also a severe indictment of the people who trampled heedlessly over Indian land and life in their rush to eat up a continent. The history of the Cherokees is not only about a great Indian nation, but also one of the dark places in the American spirit. And while these Indians have made many beginnings, so far their story has no end.

I.
The Real People

It was 1775, the eve of the white man's Revolutionary War. At a remote spot on the southeastern frontier called Sycamore Shoals in present-day Tennessee, a tall, muscular Cherokee stood up and looked at the Indians and whites seated around the council fire. His hair was raven black, and obsidian eyes glinted out from a face badly scarred by smallpox. When he began to speak, his hands accompanied his words with angry stabbing movements. After gesturing scornfully at the whites around the fire, he began to reproach the elders of his own tribe who had just taken part in the biggest land sale in frontier history. They had signed over what is today all of Kentucky and much of Tennessee to these white speculators in return for two thousand dollars and a cabin filled with cheap trading goods.

When Dragging Canoe, as whites called this man, had finished his bitter speech, he paused for a moment and then made a last prediction that one of the white men present wrote down. "Soon the whole country which the Cherokees and their fathers have so long occupied will be demanded, and the remnant of *Ani-Yun'Wiya*, The Real People, once so great and formidable, will be compelled to seek refuge in some distant wilderness . . . . Such treaties may be all right for men who are too old to hunt or fight. As for me, I have my young warriors with me. We will have our lands!" Then he stalked out, to spend the rest of his life waging war against the white settlers creeping a little farther into his people's country each day.

At the time Dragging Canoe spoke, it seemed impossible that his dismal prophecy could ever come true. The Cherokees, warlords of the Alleghenies for centuries, were still the most powerful tribe in the Southeast. They did not fear the white man now any more than they had when they first saw him.

That had been long before, in the summer of 1540, when a column of sweating soldiers had hacked their way from the Gulf Coast up to Cherokee country. Hernando de Soto and his soldiers followed the flag of Spain, the flag that came to represent bloody conquest and plunder in the Americas. They had come looking for precious metals to swell the holds of their galleons headed back to the Old World. Their tattered velvet doublets were patched with deerskin and their steel armor tarnished by tropical heat. Behind the small army trailed a herd of swine providing food for their long march. There were also nearly two hundred Indians enslaved along their route of march. They were in chains, with iron collars fastened around their necks.

De Soto was not the last explorer lured into Cherokee country by rumors of fist-sized gold nuggets lying in the open along creek beds. But like the others who came later, he found nothing. The Cherokees gave his hungry men corn and some dogs, which they—unlike the Spaniards—did not consider fit for food. There was no clash betwen the red man and the white, not this time, and these soldiers of fortune left as mysteriously as they had come. Even their memories of the powerful tribe they had stumbled across—a tribe that controlled a vast area stretching from what is today the western part of the Carolinas up to the northern border of Kentucky and down through Tennessee to northern Georgia and Alabama—were vague. The chroniclers who accompanied the DeSoto expedition forgot the meeting almost as easily as the Indians. They wrote only that the place of the Cherokees was good luck and the soldiers had found a pot of honey there.

After the forest closed upon the departing Spaniards, the Cherokees did not see whites in any numbers for another hundred years, although periodic contact with traders from St. Augustine, Florida, gave them their first guns and horses. The tribe was left as it had been for generations, since a time almost beyond memory when, according to legend, they were driven out of an earlier home in the Great Lakes area after long warfare with the Delawares and their powerful Iroquois allies. *Ani-Yun'Wiya*, as they called themselves in their own language, The Real People (the name "Cherokee" came later from the Choctaw *Chillaki* and means "cave dweller"), felt a deep reverence for their lands, which they knew had been there since the beginning even if the people had not.

The old men often told the children about the time when the world of The Real People had been created. In the beginning, they said, what is now the earth was water. The animals lived above, on a platform in the sky; but it was crowded there and they wanted to explore what was below. They sent out Water Beetle, Beaver's grandchild, to dive down into the water. He did, and after swimming down until he finally touched bottom he came up with soft mud. The animals encouraged him to dredge more of it up to the surface. He worked hard, and soon the mud began to harden a little, forming the earth's crust. The animals were anxious to go down and explore, but they were afraid that the sticky surface would not support their weight. Every day they sent out a different bird to fly down and see if it was dry yet. Finally they sent Buzzard. He flew all around, diving close to the ground with his great flapping wings. When he reached what would be the home of The Real People, he was flying so low that his wings often touched the soft earth. Where they did, a valley was indented; where he rose up, a mountain appeared. This, the old men said, is how the country of the Cherokees took its distinctive shape.

When the gods allowed them to go down to the new earth, the animals and plants—who would become the friends of The Real People—were all told to stay awake for seven nights. They tried to, but every night more of them dropped off to sleep. Of the animals, only the owl, the panther, and one or two others held out to the end. They were rewarded with the power to see at night and thus could prey on those who had fallen asleep. Of the trees, only the holly, cedar, pine, and spruce kept awake until the seventh night. Their reward was always to be green. "Because you did not endure to the end," the other trees were told, "you shall lose your hair every winter."

For The Real People land was not something to be possessed, or even "used" in the white man's sense of the word. It was to be lived on, and with an awareness that it had a spirit of its own. Every landmark had its legend. For instance, there is a cave in a high, inaccessible cliff where the Little Tennessee River bends at the mouth of Citico Creek.

The cliff hangs over some pitted rocks. This is the tale the old men told about the area.

Just after creation, a pair of giant hawks called *Tla'nuwa* came to make their nest in this cave. They terrorized the Cherokees in the village below, swooping down and seizing children in their huge talons and carrying them off to their nest. No one could climb the sheer cliff to rescue them, and the hawks scorned arrows shot up by the warriors. Finally a great medicine man decided to help the people out of their trouble. When the hawks were out hunting, he made a rope and let himself down into the cave from above. In the litter of human bones, he found their newly hatched fledglings. He picked them up and threw them down into the water below, where they were immediately swallowed up by a great serpent. When the hawks returned they were enraged over the death of their young. The male darted down to the river and speared the serpent with his talons; as he rose high in the air, his mate flew by, cutting the serpent to pieces with her beak. The hawks were so high and the serpent so huge that the pieces made holes when they dropped to the rocks. The Real People knew this place as Where Tla'nuwa Cut Up the Serpent.

Even though the Cherokees had not yet come in contact with the early English colonists, they had heard tales of these whites living near the eastern waters. The English were different from the Spaniards, other Indian tribes told them. Instead of seeking slaves or gold, they sought the land itself. They cut down forests and built towns, and even as this work was finished, some of them walked toward the setting sun and began to clear more land. The old men shook their heads. This was ominous news. The country of The Real People could not remain hidden forever.

Almost immediately after they were established, the Virginia colonists, thinking that the Indies with their fabled wealth lay just over the next mountain range, began to look westward. In 1642, their House of Burgesses passed an act giving explorers license "to discover the Mountains and Westenward parts of the Country." In 1644, construction of a series of forts on the edge of the western frontier was begun to establish a base of operations for the explorers. They also nourished a hardy breed of men who would always be ready to push forward to the next frontier. The Virginians found that the Powhatan Indians in their own colony had been right: there was no sea, and one mountain range followed another. But the dream of the Indies was quickly replaced by a new vision of limitless virgin lands, and it proved every bit as beguiling. The explorers continued to go forth, and liked what they found. In 1670, one young adventurer just returned from the edge of Cherokee lands (in what is now Kentucky) wrote "I have discovered a Country so dilitious, pleasant and fruitful that were it cultivated doubtless it would prove a Second Paradize."

The wealthier members of the new seaboard society formed land companies and were given royal charters by the English crown entitling them to huge tracts of these lands. Traders who saw that there was wealth to be gained soon became the advance guard of settlement, going among the Indians to barter kettles, axes, looking glasses, guns, and, of course, rum in return for the furs on which their New World trading empires would be built. By 1708, they counted on the Cherokees for fifty thousand skins a year; by 1730, they were taking over a million skins annually from The Real People. These Englishmen had shown that they were able to extract a land's riches more patiently than the hot-blooded Spanish conquistadors.

At the time their contact with the colonists increased, there were about twenty thousand Cherokees. William Bartram, a Philadelphia botanist who traveled through the Southeast in the 1760s, described them as being taller than other Indians of the area and lighter in complexion. The men wore breechcloths and buckskin shirts, the women skirts of calico or other trade cloth and short jackets. Both men and women wore leggings, and moccasins ornamented with porcupine quills. "In their manner and disposition they are grave and steady," Bartram wrote of the Cherokees, "honest, just and liberal, and always ready to sacrifice every pleasure, even to blood and life itself, to defend their territory and maintain their rights."

According to John Adair, a trader who went on diplomatic missions to the southeastern tribes for the English crown and later wrote one of the first histories of the American Indian, the Cherokees lived in "sixty-four towns and villages populous and full of children." There were about three hundred people in a typical town, although there were seven sacred mother towns which had as many as six hundred each. Each mother town was once the headquarters for one of the seven clans governing Cherokee social life (although by the time the white explorers arrived this was no longer true). These clans controlled marriage, kinship, and every other aspect of the society. They were responsible for the administration of justice, and the law by which they lived was based on the concept that blood must be paid for in blood. If a man who took another's life hid from vengeance, his next of kin was punished in his place by someone appointed by the elders of the clan to which the slain man had belonged.

Kituwah (near present-day Bryson City, North Carolina) was the oldest of all the mother towns and perhaps the

Cherokees' first permanent settlement in that dimly remembered time, centuries earlier, when they had migrated from the Great Lakes area to the Southeast. The tribe referred to itself occasionally as *Ani-Kituwah*, The People of Kituwah; they resurrected this sacred name later on for the resistance organizations they formed when their tribal identity was threatened time and again in the years ahead.

But in the early 1700s, The Real People had not yet realized that they, like every other Indian tribe in the New World, were destined to face the white man in a life-and-death struggle. They had not yet heard of the Powhatans, Pequots, and other eastern tribes that had already been driven to the edge of extinction by the early settlers. For a while longer the Cherokees continued to live as they always had. They were well accustomed to the other Indians of the area—especially the Creeks, Choctaws, Chickasaws, and Seminoles, who would eventually be known along with The Real People as The Five Civilized Tribes. Periodically the tribes of this area fought each other, but warfare was a training ground for warriors and these tribes did not aim for the total annihilation of enemies. The myths that had already evolved in the whites' seaboard towns were wrong: the Indians didn't scalp until the white man came with his steel knife and showed them how; the prisoners they took were as likely to experience adoption as torture; and burnings at the stake occurred less frequently than lynchings, witchcraft trials, and other barbarities in the colonies.

The Indians of the Southeast needed each other. The mountain divides were honeycombed with trails linking one tribe to another. There were native traders who went from one Nation to another, from town to town. They spoke "Mobilian," a universal Indian dialect in the Southeast, as they bartered the clay pipes from the Cherokees, garden produce from the Choctaws, and shells from the Gulf Coast tribes.

The heart of the Cherokee town was a centrally located council house, seven-sided in honor of each of the clans, built with tall log pillars and wooden crossbeams and covered with a bark roof and siding. The early English traders reported that as many as five hundred people could sit there and listen to debates on public issues that were often long and eloquent. There was also a public granary in the center of town and a communal garden where the Indians grew corn, beans, squash, and other native vegetables. Fanning out in a semicircle from the communal part of the town were individual dwellings. They were square, constructed of a framework of poles sunk in the ground, covered by bark or wood siding, and weatherproofed with clay chinking. There was a small sweathouse nearby used for purification rites and for sleeping in the coldest part of the winter.

Cherokee towns were divided into two complementary organizations called the Red and the White. White controlled the village in time of peace, with a head man (whom the Europeans insisted on calling "King" after their own fashion) presiding over council meetings and peaceful communal activities such as planting and harvesting (which were primarily the duties of women). His council of elders was composed of men from each of the clans whose hair had turned gray. They were wise men, and the description of members of a Cherokee council given years later, in 1822, by a white visitor was probably accurate for the 1700s as well. "They . . . manage their councils, and the affairs of the nation, with sober dignity, great order, deliberation and decorum," he wrote. "They proceed slowly, but surely. Nothing is permitted to interrupt their business after they engage in it; and when they have finished it, the council breaks up."

The Red organization, which took over in time of war or when the village was threatened, was more important than the White only because the tribe prided itself on its military prowess. (William Fyffe, a Charlestown planter, wrote in 1761 of the Cherokees: "Their young men are not regarded till they kill an enemy or take a prisoner. Those houses in which there's the greatest number of scalps are most honoured.") The Red organization was headed by a war chief who had proved himself in battle; he was advised by councilors of war representing the seven clans.

When a Cherokee town went from peace to war and back again, the changes were marked by ritual observance. Warriors fasted and danced to become warlike before going into battle; when they returned they underwent purification to prepare again for peaceful civic life. The alternation was presided over by the *Adawehi*, conjurors who were both priests and physicians. The Cherokees' religion was so intimately woven into the most minute aspects of their daily life that an almost invisible line separated the sacred and secular functions. The *Adawehi* wore shell necklaces with shining river pearls mounted on them as symbols that they were familiar with the secrets of the stars.

The Red and White organizations of each individual town were duplicated on a national level when the whole tribe was threatened by war or other emergency. But the Cherokees had no permanent central government, a fact that frustrated colonial traders and treaty-makers because no single person or governing group could sign the agreements these men were always anxious to make. At this time, the Cherokee nation was only the sum of its towns, and each one of them was still highly individualized, its distinct identity encouraged by town-to-town competition in events

such as the ball-play, a lacrosselike game that was the Cherokees' national sport.

In the early 1700s, when The Real People began to
come into daily contact with the colonists, their economy
revolved around hunting, fishing, and agriculture. Large
game—mainly deer, bear, and occasionally one of the buffalo
that were becoming increasingly rare in their hunting
grounds—was taken with the guns that the Indians had
obtained as a result of the fur trade. Smaller game was still
hunted by bow and arrow or blowgun, usually by children.
Of Cherokee fishing, John Adair says, "The most popular
method was to select a pool of water . . . and poison it by
means of the devil's shoestring [a native herb that acted as
a narcotic], the buckeye, or some other vegetable growth."
When the drugged fish rose to the surface, they were put
into baskets and taken to be smoked.

Cherokee life moved rhythmically in accompaniment to
the passage of time, the changes in season marked with ritual
observances celebrating the miracles of nature. There were
six festivals during the year, among them the Green Corn
Festival, which coincided with the maturity of the corn, the
staff of Cherokee life; and the New Year's Dance held late
in November when the *Adawehi*, as part of a purification
rite, put out the sacred fire that burned in each Town Council
House and started a new one on its ashes. During these times,
any friction that existed between the clans was forgotten,
those who had offended were pardoned, and The Real People
faced the future with their unity reaffirmed.

When John Adair first visited the Cherokees in 1738
he found that they had already seen enough of the white
man to have an unflattering view of him. "They frequently
tell us," he wrote, "that though we are possessed of a great
deal of yellow and white stone [gold and silver] and black

people, horses, cows, hogs, and everything else our hearts delight in—yet these things seem to create in us much toil and pain instead of ease and pleasure . . . and therefore they say we are truly poor, and deserve pity instead of envy." But their early relations with the colonists had taught The Real People to temper this pity with suspicion. As the whites penetrated deeper into the Southeast, the fragile balance which had always sustained the area was broken. Tribes which had coexisted in war and peace since their oldest men could remember, their borders having overlapped each other for centuries, were suddenly fighting over boundaries as they competed desperately for hunting and trapping grounds which would yield an ever greater number of skins and bring more of the rifles, whiskey, and cheap trade goods to which they had become addicted.

Indian was set against Indian as never before. In 1711, for instance, the Charlestown colonists had agreed to give the Cherokees guns in exchange for their help in fighting the Tuscaroras. But after the Tuscaroras were driven out, the Cherokees began to understand that the people of Charlestown had not been in jeopardy, but had stirred up the war for a deeper purpose. The leading citizens, including the governor of the colony, had given both tribes guns in exchange for the prisoners they took and delivered up. These prisoners—Tuscarora and Cherokee alike—were then sold to West Indies slave merchants.

In 1721, the Cherokees met with Charlestown's Governor Francis Nicholson to discuss this and other problems. They agreed to name a single head man with whom the colonists could negotiate and gave the English permission to send a commissioner into their towns to oversee traders. They also made their first cession of land to the whites. It was only a small and seldom-used strip on the Carolina border, but it was a fateful moment in the history of The Real People, for it marked the beginning of a process that would eventually swallow up every acre they possessed and send them off to an unknown land.

In 1730, another milestone was passed when an Englishman named Sir Alexander Cuming visited the Cherokees and urged them to acknowledge the sovereignty of the King of England. He told them that by swearing allegiance to the Great White Father Across the Sea, they would increase the flow of trade goods and the hostility that divided them from the Charlestown colonists would disappear. Cuming conceived the idea of taking some of the Indians to England, and that year he set sail for the Old World with seven Cherokees, including the small chief named Attakullaculla (called "Little Carpenter" by the whites because he was such a skillful diplomat that he was said to be able to make every joint and corner of an agreement meet perfectly).

When the Cherokees arrived in London, they were shown all the fashionable spots and had their portraits done in their new broadcloth suits. Even though groups of Indians had been brought to England since Sir Walter Raleigh first explored the New World for his Queen Elizabeth, these Cherokees were still a great curiosity. Crowds followed them and they were even exhibited without their knowledge by unscrupulous innkeepers who charged the curious a fee to peep through curtains at the red men sitting unaware in their rooms. They had an audience with King George II, and agreed to trade only with the English, to allow no other whites in their country, and to give up to English law white lawbreakers fleeing to their country. In return, the English offered protection and friendship, as the agreement said, "for as long as the mountains and rivers last, and the sun shines." This was the kind of language the Cherokees could understand, and they returned home as eager to tell about the strange land and customs they had discovered as Columbus's sailors had been to tell of the New World they had stumbled upon. But if they had gained a Great White Father, they had also lost a portion of their freedom.

In 1738 the Cherokees were struck by smallpox, a catastrophe that decimated the other Indian nations as well. There is strong evidence that whites used this dread disease as an early form of germ warfare in their relations with some eastern tribes, spreading it by the gift of blankets that had been exposed to the disease. But the Cherokees got smallpox that had been incubated in the filthy holds of the slave ships docked at Charlestown harbor with their black cargo, and then spread like wildfire through the whole of the Southeast, a symbol of the moral infection slavery was bringing to the New World.

The *Adawehi* had a pharmacology of folk medicine for other ailments. (Adair notes that the Cherokees, "like other Indian Nations, have a great knowledge of herbs and plants . . . and seldom if ever fail to effect a cure from Nature's bush.") The old men taught that in the beginning the animals had once rebelled against man, and in a solemn council each had devised an affliction to visit upon the humans who had killed them so mercilessly; but the plants, always friendly to man, had agreed to provide a remedy for each of the diseases the animals brought. Thus when a man had rheumatism in his joints, the *Adawehi* would give him the maidenhair fern to chew on: just as the fronds of the plant straightened out as it grew, so the aching muscles of the man who ate it would relax.

But this kind of medicine was of no use against smallpox. Purification in the sacred sweatbath only made it worse; even eating the flesh of the buzzard, whose foul smell was thought to keep all illness-producing spirits at bay, was useless. The Cherokees, as one Indian put it, "died like rotten sheep." When John Adair stayed with them a few years after the epidemic, he learned that some warriors who had survived the disease committed suicide after they happened to glimpse their scarred and disfigured features in a mirror. In all, one-half of the entire Cherokee people perished from smallpox in less than a year.

They were just recovering from this catastrophe when the French and Indian War broke out in 1754. The Virginia colony feared the French would move into the rich Ohio valley which it claimed as its own western lands, and The Real People, like other tribes, were caught up in the struggle of these two European powers for control of the wealth of the New World. The Cherokees allied themselves with the English colonists, whose traders had become essential to them. The colonists well appreciated that the Indians could tilt the balance of power. George Washington, then a lieutenant colonel in the militia, had written Virginia's Governor Dinwiddie of the Cherokees fighting on the English side: "They are more serviceable than twice their number of white men. . . . If they return to their nation, no words can tell how much they will be missed."

The only problem was that the English often didn't bother to distinguish their Indian allies from their Indian enemies. And in 1756 when a war party of Cherokees was passing through Virginia's back country on the way home after a campaign against the French, they were ambushed by settlers lured on by the £15 reward the Virginia colony had offered for any Indian scalp. In all twenty-four of the

Cherokees were killed. From then on, the Cherokees continued to go out against the French enemies of the Great White Father Across the Sea, but they had begun to see that the frontiersmen were their real enemies, and they burned cabins and fields and killed whites when they could. Two years later, one of their war chiefs killed twenty-four South Carolina settlers in final repayment for the ambush. Even the diplomatic Little Carpenter was hard-pressed to prevent total war from breaking out along the length of the frontier.

Up to the early 1760s, the colonists had been too busy struggling with the French and other nations to encroach very seriously on the Cherokees' lands. But the final settlement of the French and Indian War in the 1763 Treaty of Paris gave England title to all American lands east of the Mississippi. This was a spur to white settlement. It helped create the vision of an open frontier and the free land that became so much a part of the American dream. But in order that this dream could come true, Indians would have to be dispossessed—by treaty, if possible, by warfare if that failed —and so in 1775 the Cherokees found themselves at Sycamore Shoals negotiating a huge land sale with a group of private speculators calling themselves the Transylvania Land Company.

Most of the headmen were willing to sign the agreement, except the fiercely independent Dragging Canoe, surrounded by Doublehead, Pumpkin Boy, Bloody Fellow, and other warriors whose names would soon strike terror into the hearts of white settlements. Dragging Canoe said that whites were pushing into the lands of The Real People from all sides and that the tribe must now make a stand before it was too late. Even his father, the ninety-year-old Little Carpenter, listened with his head bowed in shame. But the negotiations had gone too far to turn back now, and the agreement was signed. As he gathered his warriors around him, Dragging Canoe looked at the whites and said, "You will find the settlement of this land dark and bloody."

Like other Indians, the Cherokees had trouble understanding the Revolutionary War. Why would brothers of the same tribe speaking the same language kill each other so remorselessly? Early in 1775, the Continental Congress had sent word of the impending conflict to several Indian tribes, saying: "This is a family quarrel between us and old England. We desire you to remain at home and not join on either side, but to keep the hatchet buried deep." But for Dragging Canoe and his supporters, it was a situation to be exploited. They recognized that one of the basic issues involved, despite the colonists' passionate talk about liberty, was a conflict between two different ways of regarding the New World. To the English it was primarily an area producing revenue for the crown. But those defying the redcoats saw it as a place to be settled, controlled, and populated—not merely to have its wealth sent abroad. Although most of the tribe's leaders remained neutral, Dragging Canoe (with about one fourth of the Cherokees) allied himself with the English, taking their guns and ammunition and continuing his fight against the colonists.

Although they did not fight the colonists, the rest of the tribe saw them as a danger. Old Tassel, a leader of the tribe's peace group, wrote the governor of South Carolina in clear terms: "BROTHER: We are a poor distressed people that is in great trouble . . . . We have no place to hunt on. Your people have built houses within a day's walk of our towns. We don't want to quarrel with our Elder Brother. We therefore hope our Elder Brother will not take our lands from us that the Great Man above gave us. We are the first people that ever lived on this land. It is ours."

If the Cherokees hadn't known before that they were on a collision course with the whites, they soon did, for the Virginia and Carolina colonists raised militia and set out to completely destroy the tribe. In the year 1776 alone, scores of Cherokee towns were devastated and hundreds of people killed, most of them scalped on the spot. Those captured were often auctioned off as slaves. In one instance Virginia soldiers sold a pair of women and a child for twelve hundred dollars. The South Carolina legislature offered seventy-five dollars for the scalps of warriors and a higher bounty on those taken alive.

Dragging Canoe and his warriors (called "Chickamaugans" because their base of operations was the Chickamaugua Creek area in Georgia) fought bitterly against the frontiersmen, not pausing when the Revolutionary War had ended; but the main body of the Cherokees still tried to maintain a tentative peace. When Little Carpenter died, Old Tassel (who once perceptively told fawning representatives of the new American union, "We should have fewer friends if we had fewer lands") became the leading peace chief. He faced a new colonial government that wasn't sure how to deal with Indians—whether to give authority to the states or keep it for itself—and couldn't determine how to reestablish the intricate trade network that had collapsed when the English withdrew.

In 1785 the Cherokees made the Treaty of Hopewell, their first treaty with the United States. In return for more lands, the government set out what were to be the formal boundaries of the Cherokees' land and stated that they would be respected and that no further white intrusion would be tolerated. But there were already over three thousand whites living illegally on Cherokee lands. The U.S. took no steps to expel them, but Dragging Canoe did; he and his warriors made constant raids on the frontier cabins that were thrown up overnight and chased off the surveyors busily laying out lands they didn't own. The Indians seized their compasses, which they called Land Stealers, and smashed them against the trees.

The frontier war continued for years, often involving those Cherokees who tried to keep the peace as well as Dragging Canoe and his Chickamaugans. Finally President George Washington became concerned. Such wars were not only costly but were not in keeping with the new republic's view of itself. Also, the fact that the settlers were so brazenly disregarding the Treaty of Hopewell was a threat to the federal government's authority to regulate Indian affairs. In 1791 therefore, he persuaded the Cherokees to sign the new Treaty of Holston. It gave the United States the sole right to trade with Indians and prohibited them from having diplomatic relations with other countries; in return, it once again forbade further trespass on Cherokee lands and agreed to give the tribe a thousand-dollar yearly payment to compensate for lands that had been taken. But the clause in the treaty that came to be most significant read: "That the Cherokee Nation may be led to a greater degree of civilization, and to become herdsmen and cultivators, instead of remaining in a state of hunters, the United States will from time to time furnish . . . useful implements of husbandry."

In 1792, after a band of frontiersmen crossed over into Cherokee Territory, destroyed six towns, and took fifteen scalps, Doublehead and other Chickamaugan warriors retaliated by burning a small settlement near present-day Knox-ville, Tennessee, killing eighteen people. But such warfare could only be a rear-guard action. It seemed that nothing the Indians did could keep their lands free from the whites. The peace leaders of the tribe had signed treaties in an attempt to establish a buffer zone between them and the advancing tide of settlement. The war party had fought fire with fire. Neither strategy had worked. The Cherokee warriors were diminished by disease and a generation of fighting; the tribe saw the stark truth: they were limited while the whites were numberless. Something new must be tried.

More than sixty years old and partly crippled from wounds received in his long war with the white man, Dragging Canoe died in March 1792, a year after the Treaty of Holston was signed. He received a chief's burial: his body was washed and dressed in his best clothes; his hair was anointed with oil and his face painted red one last time. He was placed in the ground, facing the rising sun.

The old ways were dying with him, and the Cherokees were about to step over into a new world. But Dragging Canoe's prophecy of twenty years earlier—that The Real People would someday be driven to a distant wilderness—was a legacy for the future.

II.
The Sheep
and the Wolves

By making a compromise with slavery and specifying in their Constitution that a slave was equal to three-fifths a white man, the founding fathers pushed aside the issue that would someday tear the United States in half. For the time being, the Indian seemed to pose a greater problem than the human chattel docking every day at Charleston and other American ports. The first philosophers of the new republic spent as much time defending the dispossession of the red man as their descendants did rationalizing the brutal treatment of the black.

For some, of course, the "Indian question" was easily answered. An influential Pennsylvania writer named Hugh Brackenridge had spoken for many when he said in 1782 that "the animals, vulgarly called Indians," should be "exterminated." But this was too bloodthirsty a view for the patricians in control of colonial government, and John Adams for one had approached the issue more discreetly. "What is the right of the huntsman to the thousand miles over which he has accidentally ranged in quest of prey?" he asked. "Shall the liberal bounties of Providence to the race of man be monopolized by one or two thousand?"

The Indian was disinherited not because he was an animal, but because the whites felt they had better claim to his holdings. It was his lands the Americans wanted, not his life, although they wouldn't hesitate to take that too if he resisted. How did the whites justify taking over the continent? By saying they were "more civilized" than the Indian, and therefore could put the land to better "use" than he did. Whites built towns where the word of God was heard, while the Indian was a heathen. They farmed in closely furrowed acres, while the red man needed a wide expanse of virgin territory to hunt for game. Even as late as 1900, when some white Americans felt conscience-stricken over the brutality used against Indians in previous centuries, this reasoning surfaced once again in Teddy Roosevelt's cold statement: "The settler and pioneer have at bottom had justice on their side; this great continent could not have been kept as nothing but a game preserve for squalid savages."

There was something else in the back of many Americans' minds. Since the Revolutionary War, the Appalachian mountain range and even the mighty Mississippi River no longer seemed the natural boundaries limiting expansion. Soon Americans began to talk about their special duty—later on it would be called their "manifest destiny"—to populate the lands to the west. This belief that whites had a holy mission in the New World went back to the early 1600s when the Puritans landed on its rocky shores and quoted the Bible to justify taking what had been the Indians'. John Winthrop, Governor of the Massachusetts Colony, wrote: "The whole earth is the Lord's Garden & He hath given it to the Sons of Men with a general condition, Genesis I, 28: increase & multiply, replenish and subdue it . . . . And for the Natives of New England, they enclose no land, neither have they any settled habitation, nor any cattle to improve the land by . . . ." After a while it was not necessary to cite scripture or engage in theological argument to justify taking Indian lands, for the idea of an expanding America became inseparable from the idea of America itself.

In the early days of the new republic, however, the Cherokees were as yet a powerful people and the government could not afford to anger them needlessly. Therefore, during a brief period following the Treaty of Holston, they were dealt with even-handedly. When this treaty was being negotiated, Secretary of War Henry Knox wrote President Washington a letter containing simple words which could have been the basis for a just Indian policy: "The Indians, being prior occupants, possess the right of the soil. It cannot be taken from them unless by their consent . . . ." The red man still presented a problem, however, since white settlers constantly spilled over every border established by treaties. Something had to be done to prevent conflict, so Knox had conceived the strategy of offering Indians agricultural tools and instruction in their use. This would indirectly serve the settler by getting tribes to restrict themselves to smaller plots of land; but it also affirmed the fact that the land did belong to the Indians.

The Cherokees took the Secretary of War at his word. The tribe recognized that it had reached a crossroads. One way—the path Henry Knox beckoned them to—perhaps led toward the unknown, but the other—the path of continued conflict—led only to extinction. It was possible that the Americans meant what they said about the red and white men living together in mutual toleration. The Real People dropped their weapons and picked up the plowshare offered them. Even Bloody Fellow, once one of Dragging Canoe's fiercest Chickamaugan warriors, went as part of a delegation to meet Secretary Knox in 1792 and told him, "The treaty mentions ploughs, hoes, cattle, and other things for a farm; this is what we want; game is going fast away among us. We must plant corn and raise cattle . . . ." The Cherokees decided to take the new path not because the white ways were better, but because they felt the dagger at their throat.

The Cherokee towns had always had communal gardens of squash, pumpkin, corn, and other native crops, but almost overnight farms like those of their white neighbors sprang up on Indian land. Cherokee women began to work the looms given them by Indian agents, who—as stipulated in the Treaty of Holston—lived among The Real People and brought tools and craftsmen to teach them skills. Slowly and ingeniously the tribe began to reshape the course of its history. The equipment and techniques may have been supplied by the whites, but the way they were used was dictated by the full-blood chiefs. For instance, whites had been asking permission for years to come among the Cherokees, set up schools, and spread the white man's gospel. In 1801, when the Council of Chiefs and Warriors finally allowed Moravian missionaries to establish the first such school in Cherokee country, they did so only because they knew that the next generation of children must have the white man's book learning if they were to cope with his schemes to take their land. When the missionaries came and began only to seek religious converts, the old men of the tribe said sternly, "We have no ears to hear it," and gave them six months to show they could succeed in teaching the three R's.

In 1744, a Virginia tribe had replied to the colonists'

offer to educate their children by saying that Indians who attended white schools returned home "bad runners, ignorant of every means of living in the woods, unable to bear the cold or hunger; they knew neither how to build a cabin, how to take a deer or kill an enemy . . . and were therefore neither fit for hunters, warriors or councillors. They were totally good for nothing." But times had changed, and now it was necessary to resist the white man with his own tools, particularly by learning to read the books and writings old men called "the talking leaves." The Moravians and other missionaries who came among the Cherokees fulfilled their part of the bargain, and the Cherokee children took giant steps in the small one-room schoolhouses that sprang up like wild flowers across the frontier. Even local whites like Tennessee's John Sevier, an old Indian fighter who had battled the Cherokees for years (and who had once justified killing Indian women and children with the famous remark, "Nits make lice"), had to admit that the progress was amazing.

By 1808, the Cherokee Council had also begun to centralize its informal government, about which one missionary had written: "It is a government in which there are no positive laws, only established habits and customs; no code of jurisprudence, but the experience of former times; no magistrates but advisors to whom the people nevertheless pay a willing obedience, in which age confers rank, wisdom gives power, and moral goodness secures a title to universal respect." But what was adequate for the old ways would not serve the new ones. In 1809, the Cherokees adopted written laws, substituted trials before the Council for the old blood law of the clans, provided for the taxation of those owning livestock, and introduced a system of law enforcement with Indian sheriffs ranging throughout the countryside. The individual towns which had controlled the life of the people for generations began to be less important than before. The nucleus of a centralized Cherokee Nation emerged out of a coalition of past and future.

As these changes were taking place, two remarkable men were assuming positions of leadership in the new Nation. One was a full blood called The Ridge. He had been born in 1771 with a longer name, which translated as Man Who Walks on Mountain Top, in a small, traditional Cherokee town on the Hiwassee River in present-day Tennessee. When his portrait was painted in the 1820s by a white artist traveling through Cherokee country, The Ridge was still robust and handsome, his broad face set off by a shock of wavy white hair. He wore a well-tailored suit of broadcloth and a starched ruffled collar at his neck. He lived in a large and lavishly furnished house with hundreds of acres under cultivation. By then he was one of the most eloquent orators among the Cherokees, and one of the most respected leaders. But The Ridge had started life as a warrior and a hunter. He had taken white scalps in Doublehead's war with the white settlers. His development paralleled that of his people.

Some full bloods turned their backs on the civilization program, suspecting that it would be the final step in the destruction of the old ways that had guided the people. But even though he had no schooling or formal education, The Ridge saw early in his life that adaptation to some white ways did not mean giving up the traditions and culture of The Real People. Just as certain animals took on the color of their surroundings to hide from predators, so the Cherokees would use appearances to protect their old ways.

When The Ridge was married, it may be that he formalized the betrothal in the traditional Cherokee way, killing a deer and taking it to the door of his bride's parents to prove that he would be a good provider. But soon after he moved to a log house and was at work clearing broad acres with the farming implements sent in under the plan of Henry Knox. His children spent their early years wandering through the forests with blowguns and digging for crayfish in the rivers, but they received a good education; and especially the frail and intelligent son, John Ridge, seemed marked for greatness.

The Ridge came to the Council and helped convince the Cherokee elders to set aside the old blood law of clan vengeance. Later on, he counseled the tribe to enter the Creek War of 1812 on the side of the Americans. He saw the imperative facing his people—change or die—and became a leading spokesman for the new ways. His fate was intimately interwoven with that of the Nation he served all his life, and his own tragedy, which would one day strike this Nation like lightning, highlighted the catastrophe that eventually befell all the people.

When full bloods like The Ridge were taking the tribe on its first tentative steps along the white man's path, they were aided by a different class of Cherokees that had emerged as a result of contact with the whites. By the turn of the century mixed-blood Cherokees constituted an important force within the Nation. Throughout the mid-1700s white traders had come among the tribe and gained a place in its life by bartering their wares in exchange for furs. Generally, they were Scotch and Irish adventurers who had journeyed to the New World and found the English-oriented seaboard society almost as closed to them as London had been. They were not unlike the Europeans who came to America a century later to escape famine and hardship only to become trapped in factories and big-city slums. But these earlier immigrants found that American society of the 1700s, especially along the untrammeled frontier, still had room for newcomers. As a practical matter, these merchant adventurers couldn't afford the usual colonial prejudices against the Indian; but for other reasons as well, many of them married into the tribes they did business with.

The children of these marriages grew up among the Cherokees. Part white and part Indian, many of them spent a lifetime trying to figure out their racial allegiances. Because of the wealth their white fathers had accumulated from trading, many mixed bloods were able to go north for their schooling. They mastered the white man's manners and language and learned to move with ease in his society. When they came back home from school many of them (now more "white" than Indian) drifted off to become part of the frontier society in the new states being carved out of the wilderness. But some remained behind. These mixed bloods were destined to play a crucial role in tribal affairs, especially in the days ahead when their sophistication and learning, and their understanding of white ways, became an invaluable weapon in the Cherokees' fight to keep their homeland. But the mixed bloods, in keeping with their ambiguous status, were a problem as well as an asset. Especially after submitting to the white man's God, they could no longer believe in the old Cherokee myths by which the people had lived for centuries; their wealth and property made them conceive of the tribe more as a voluntary collection of individuals than as a functioning community with needs of its own. In many cases, the mixed bloods' white heritage asserted itself and some came to see themselves as an educated elite whose background and wealth made them superior to the full blood and more capable of guiding the tribe's destiny. When this happened some of them unknowingly became as dangerous to the full blood—who continued to be loyal to the old ways of The Real People—as the white man. But there were exceptions, men among the mixed bloods who served the wishes of the tribe as a whole. John Ross was such a man.

Ross's grandfather, John MacDonald, was born in Scotland in 1747. After visiting London, he decided to journey to the New World and arrived in Charleston in 1776 as a clerk in a company trading with Cherokees. He was sent to Fort Loundon, one of the outposts the English had built on Cherokee land near the Tennessee River, and while there, he married a Cherokee woman, was accepted by the Indians, and eventually settled down to open his own trading company in northern Georgia.

Daniel Ross, also a Scot, had come to America at the beginning of the Revolutionary War. Filling a flatboat with merchandise, he began to float down the Tennessee River in hopes of reaching the country of the Chickasaws, where he planned to trade his goods for furs. But on the way he ran into one of Dragging Canoe's war parties. He would have been killed on the spot except that John MacDonald happened along and rescued him. Daniel Ross stayed with MacDonald, married his daughter, and eventually won the Cherokees' permission to remain among them as a trader.

John Ross was born in Tennessee in 1790, the third of nine children. Although only one-eighth Cherokee, he grew up more like a full blood than mixed blood, resisting most of his parents' attempts to "civilize" him. When he was seven years old, they took him to a Green Corn Festival, the annual gathering of the clans to celebrate Nature's goodness in ripening the corn. It was the best time of the year for an Indian boy. He could eat all he wanted, watch the solemn *Adawehi* carrying gourd shakers adorned with rattlesnake rattles, and see the greatest athletes in the Nation strip to the waist and compete in the ball-play. In the evening, graceful dancers coiled back and forth in the Green Corn Dance, and the old men told tales about olden times. But for the first time John Ross was forced by his parents to wear the white man's clothes, the homespun suit that itched and the heavy shoes that cramped his feet. His friends began to tease him, derisively calling him *Unaka*, white boy. After a few minutes, he went back to his parents' house and refused to go outside again until he was allowed to throw off the stiff store-bought clothes and put back on his buckskin hunting shirt, leggings, and moccasins.

A rather short young man (he was affectionately called *Tsan Usdi*, "Little John," by the people), Ross had his father's blue eyes and thick brown hair. He received a good education at an academy in Kingston, Tennessee, where he lived with one of his father's friends. When he wasn't in school, the young man often sat on the porch and sadly watched the torrent of settlers rolling through town in covered wagons on their way to Indian country.

At the age of twenty-two, Ross went as ambassador of the tribe on a hazardous keelboat trip up the Arkansas to talk with Cherokees who had moved across that river, escaping the civilization program and the intrusion of the white man into their country. After that he traveled throughout the Nation for three years on trading expeditions for his father before becoming a leading figure in the Cherokee Council. He already showed signs of the steadiness and quiet power that led a U.S. Army general to remark of him decades later, "although not a fluent speaker, even in conversation, Ross is a clear-minded, accurate thinker of very far-reaching views." If John Ross was unlike other mixed bloods, it was because early in life he had come to believe that the full-blood Cherokees living in small towns were the heart of the tribe and he felt that a leader must serve their vision.

As the Cherokees gradually exchanged their breechcloths for leather shirts and their traditional dwellings for sturdy log cabins, the handful of missionaries, Indian agents, and traders living among them in the early 1800s began to send home astonished reports about what was taking place. To the whites' amazement, the Indian culture was being transformed overnight. After describing how schools and agriculture had taken hold and how the leaders of the tribe had begun to change their government and adopt laws resembling those of their white neighbors, one missionary wrote in 1808: "Thus far are the Cherokees advanced; farther I believe than any other nation or tribe in America."

But contrary to their hopes, The Real People's alteration in their pattern of life had not lessened the whites' desire for their lands. After George Washington's presidency, the central feature of the government's Indian policy—saying one thing and doing another—began to develop. When faced with the conflict between the treaty rights of the red man as "prior occupants" and the pressure to expand, the United States chose expansion (leading Abraham Lincoln to remark later on, "The love of property and the consciousness of right and wrong have different places in our organization."). The maps made in the early 1800s—with the purchases, territories, and claims colored in different shades—suggest that the making of America was the work of a shrewd Yankee real estate developer. These maps gave no hint of the chaos into which whole nations of people were plunged as a result of the bargaining.

Some men whose policies most hurt the Indians appeared

to be most enlightened. Thomas Jefferson scorned Indian-haters who insisted that the red men were "animals." He believed that every man was "endowed by nature with rights and an innate sense of justice; he claimed to be fearful of what would happen when the white man became the protector of his red brother. "The sheep are happier of themselves than under the care of wolves," he once said. But the Indians posed a political problem, and during his administration Jefferson decided that the best solution would be to intensify the pressure to make them farmers. "When the Indians withdraw to the culture of a small piece of land," he wrote, "they will perceive how useless to them are the extensive forests and will be willing to pare them off from time to time in exchange for necessities for their farms and families." Ultimately, Jefferson believed, they would completely intermarry with whites and be assimilated.

"It is essential to cultivate their love," Jefferson always insisted. "All our liberalities to them must proceed from pure humanity only." But as his arch enemy Alexander Hamilton said, Jefferson was not a man to let his theories stand in the way of practical matters. (And as critics then and since have pointed out, Jefferson was allowed the leisure to speculate on human freedom because he was supported by three generations of slaves.) Beneath the philosophical facade, when it came to actually dealing with the Indians, what he wanted was the same as the average settler: the red man's land. He was so anxious to consolidate the lands east of the Mississippi for the federal government that he could sound bloodthirsty on occasion. Indians were in the way, and during the border wars of 1776, he had said of them: "Nothing will reduce those wretches so soon as pushing the war into the heart of their country. But I would not stop there. I would never cease pursuing while one of them remained on this side of the Mississippi." Later, he wrote: "Should any tribe be foolhardy enough to take up the hatchet, the seizing of the whole country of that tribe and driving them across the Mississippi as the only condition of peace would be an example to others and a furtherance of our final consolidation . . . ."

It was during the Jefferson administration (1801–09) that the first serious consideration was given to simply uprooting Indian nations from their ancestral lands and removing them across the Mississippi. The President claimed that such a move was humane: it would benefit the tribes by giving them vast domains where they could continue to live as hunters; it would also take them far from the corrupting influence of whites. It was Jefferson who conceived the idea of setting up government stores, called "factories," among the southeastern tribes and encouraging them to buy trade goods on credit. After getting the Indians "and especially their leading men to run in debt . . . beyond their individual means of paying," the President said that what he called their "primitive honesty" would work to the government's advantage. "Whenever in that situation they will always cede land to rid themselves of the debt."

Another of his techniques for obtaining Indian lands was to have his Indian agents bribe leading chiefs to sign treaties containing land cessions. For a while this worked, but finally it led to a dramatic event which burned itself deeply into the imagination of The Real People and strengthened their determination to protect their lands.

In 1806, the volatile Doublehead, a fiery warrior who had followed Dragging Canoe, was approached by one of Jefferson's agents and persuaded to sign away three large and valuable tracts of the tribe's Tennessee lands in return for money and the promise of two choice pieces of a square mile each for himself and his family. This was not the first time he had cooperated with agents, and, finding out what he had done, the Cherokee elders determined that he had committed an unforgivable treason and should die. The Ridge and a mixed blood named Alexander Saunders were selected as his assassins.

They rode to the government's Indian agency at Hiwassee and waited for Doublehead in a tavern. It was late in the day when he arrived, half drunk and excited. He had just come from a ball-play where he had shot and killed an Indian named Bonepolisher, who had accused him of treason during a violent quarrel over signing away tribal lands. Doublehead came in brushing the red dust from his clothes and sat down at a table. The two executioners watched him as he called for a bottle and poured himself a drink. Then The Ridge calmly pulled a gun from his belt, walked over, and shot Doublehead in the face. As he slumped to the floor, blood spurting from his shattered jaw, The Ridge and Saunders made their escape. Later that night they found out that Doublehead was not dead, but lay wounded in the loft of a nearby cabin. They tracked him there and quietly climbed up the ladder. When they threw open the door, giving out a shrill war whoop, the wounded man leaped up and tried to wrestle the gun out of The Ridge's hand. Saunders came up with a tomahawk and drove it so deeply into Doublehead's skull that he had to use two hands and his knee as a brace to pry it out. Afterward, The Ridge spoke to the crowd of Indians who had gathered, and explained why such a sale of the Nation's lands had to be punished by death.

During these turbulent times, President Jefferson continued to graciously receive Cherokee delegations at the White House. Despite the use of "factories" and bribery to acquire their lands, he assured the Indians that he would treat them honorably, and encouraged them to continue along the road of progress. But in these conferences Jefferson failed to tell the Cherokees that he had already made an ominous agreement—the 1802 Compact—with the state of Georgia.

With his keen eye for land values, the President was able to obtain for the federal government all the western lands Georgia claimed—an area that would eventually become the states of Alabama and Mississippi—in exchange for $1,250,000 and the promise to extinguish all Indian titles inside Georgia's borders. The agreement seemed quite vague at the time. There were no deadlines set, and the Cherokees were never consulted. No one imagined that the Georgia Compact would eventually set the stage for one of the greatest tragedies ever to befall an Indian tribe in America and go far to justify Jefferson's later remark—although in ways he didn't dream of—"Indeed, I tremble for my country when I reflect that God is just."

In 1811, after Thomas Jefferson had retired to Monticello to devote the rest of his life to philosophy, an Indian with a remarkable vision appeared among the Cherokees and other southeastern tribes. He was tall and sinewy, with hollow cheeks and a hooked nose. Although educated by a white tutor, he wore plain buckskin and had a tomahawk and hunting knife tucked into the belt cinched around his waist. He was Tecumseh, the great Shawnee chief, whose dream was to weld all the Indian tribes into a union capable of stopping the white invaders and, under the religious leadership of his brother (called The Prophet), return to the old ways. Although his dream hadn't come to pass when he died in battle fighting against the Americans as a British officer in the War of 1812, Tecumseh did manage to build an impressive

Indian confederacy that encompassed thirty-two tribes at the height of its power.

It was at a meeting in the Great Smoky Mountains that Tecumseh, who had already spent years working toward his Indian confederacy, addressed a Cherokee Council. His braided hair was decorated with a white crane feather and one that had been dyed vermilion. Scarlet paint flared down along his cheekbones and was patterned on his chest. He stood silhouetted against the fire that sent smoke up into the chill November evening. "Once we owned the land from the sunrise to the sunset," he began, "once our campfires twinkled at night like the stars of a fallen sky. Then the white man came. Everywhere our people have passed away as the snow melts in May. We no longer rule the forest. The game are gone like our hunting grounds. Even our lands are nearly gone. Yes, my brothers, our campfires are few. Those that still burn we must draw together. Behold what the white man has done to our people. Gone are the Pequot, the Narragansett, the Powhatan, the Tuscarora, and the Coree. They have put their sand upon them and they are no more. We can no longer trust the white man. We gave him our tobacco and our maize. What happened? Now there is hardly land for us to grow these holy plants. Soon there will be no place for the Cherokee to hunt the deer and bear. The tomahawk of the Shawnee is ready. Will the Cherokee raise the tomahawk? Will the Cherokee join their brothers the Shawnee?"

The young men seized their weapons and shouted agreement. The honor of The Real People was not dead. The white man could be driven out of their country and back into the sea where he had come from. But then the old Cherokee chief Junaluska, after glancing at the other elders sitting cross-legged around the fire, rose and shook his head.

Looking at Tecumseh, he said wistfully: "We have learned with sorrow it is better not to war against our white brothers. We know they have come to stay. They are like the leaves in the forest, they are so many. We believe we can live in peace with them." The Cherokees feared that not even a mighty union of tribes could defeat the whites. At any rate, they were too affected by the white man's culture to turn back now. In their hearts, even the hot-blooded young men knew this.

When Tecumseh left the Council in the Great Smoky Mountains, he journeyed farther south to ask the Creeks to prepare for a day of judgment when all red men would rise up. There his message fell on more responsive ears. Traditionalists—called "Red Sticks" because of the vermilion markings on their war clubs—were strong in the Creek tribe; they outnumbered those who like the Cherokees were committed to walking the road of the white. They were ready to take up arms one last time to protect the old ways. In 1812, not long after Tecumseh left them, these Red Sticks declared war against progressives in the tribe, burning their farms and destroying livestock and other symbols of the white man's civilization. Gradually this conflict enlarged beyond Creek borders as the fierce warriors attacked the stockades American settlers had built on lands which were theirs.

The Creek War of 1812–'13 gave the federal government a chance to claim formally lands into which whites had already spilled while putting down what it called a dangerous insurrection. It was also a fateful event for the Cherokees, who found themselves caught in a moral dilemma. They were the Creeks' neighbors and friends, but the U.S. government demanded that they choose sides. After much deliberation, with The Ridge playing a dominant role, they decided to fight alongside the white man: if the Red

43

Sticks' war spread into Cherokee lands, it would ruin their experiment with the white man's ways. As The Real People raised a company of volunteers to fight, their destiny intersected for the first time with that of Andrew Jackson, who would remain their nemesis until they had been sent across The Trail of Tears and he was a gaunt old man dying at his Hermitage.

Jackson had not yet won his reputation as a leader of the coonskin Democrats who would one day sweep him to the presidency; but he had distinguished himself as an Indian fighter and bitter opponent of the red man. As a freshman congressman from the new state of Tennessee, he had risen in 1796 to disagree with President Washington's Indian policies, saying that it was better to beat concessions out of them than to draw up treaties. He even hinted that President Washington should be impeached for not being sufficiently warlike where "savages" were concerned. Jackson never made any apologies for this position: not only had he been involved in the frontier wars against the Indians but he had speculated with their land as well, having purchased some thirty thousand acres of it for pennies an acre, then resold it at a large profit, the kind of dealings that were later prohibited by Washington's Treaty of Holston.

Jackson took command of the Tennessee militia that gathered to subdue the Creeks. Several hundred Cherokees marched with him, wearing two feathers in a headband with a deer's tail trailing down their back to distinguish them from the hostiles. For some time, the Creek War went badly for Jackson; his forces were unable to decisively defeat the Red Sticks, and in some cases narrowly avoided defeat themselves. Then they met a body of over one thousand Creeks massed in upper Alabama at a sharp bend in the Tallapoosa River known as the Horseshoe. There, in a pitched battle of several hours on a river delta, the Red Sticks were slaughtered, fewer than one hundred of them surviving. Cherokee warriors had helped tip the scale in Andrew Jackson's favor. After the Battle of Horseshoe Bend, his reputation as a brilliant commander was insured.

Major Ridge (The Ridge attained the rank of major in the Creek War and afterward adopted this title as a first name) and the other Cherokees had been cautioned by their white leaders not to engage in battlefield barbarities. But even the wildest stories of Indian savagery hardly equaled what they witnessed: the white soldiers wandered over the area where the Creeks lay, snipping off their noses to establish a body count and occasionally pausing to skin a corpse to make purses and other mementos. There was also the grotesque spectacle—recalled later on by the legendary Davy Crockett, who had been at the Horseshoe—of the soldiers roasting potatoes basted in oil drippings from the skin of Creeks who had fought from inside a blockhouse and been incinerated there when it was set on fire.

If these sights sickened the Cherokee volunteers and made them wonder if the path they had chosen was really the path of civilization, they had even more cause to regret helping the Americans when they got home. During their absence white settlers had plundered their lands, stolen livestock, destroyed their crops, and set fire to some of their villages. And it became clear in the aftermath of the war that the Americans were going to try for a territorial adjustment that would involve the holdings of Cherokee allies as well as the Creek enemies.

Jackson got himself appointed to the U.S. Commission in charge of redrawing borders to punish the Creeks for their insurrection. He not only demanded some 23 million acres from the Creek nation, but also tried to include some of the

Cherokees' Tennessee lands as well. When they held fast, he resorted to the old technique of bribery, offering what was then the princely sum of $4,250 to one chief and $1,000 to another, as one Indian agent wrote, "to stop his mouth and attain his consent." This resulted in a small land cession in the treaty Jackson finally negotiated with the Cherokees in 1817, although his cavalier attitude toward such a document was clear in the words he wrote President Monroe the same year: "I have long viewed treaties with Indians as an absurdity not to be reconciled with principles of government."

In getting this piece of Cherokee land, Jackson used as his lever the fact that some twenty-five hundred Cherokees deeply opposed to the adoption of white culture had been emigrating voluntarily to Arkansas over the years. Jackson argued that a cession of land should be made to compensate the government for the lands these Indians (known as the "Old Settlers") now occupied. Meanwhile, he also maneuvered to get even more Cherokees to join them, having inherited Jefferson's dream of moving all Indians across the Mississippi. The Commission of which Jackson was a part offered any Cherokee who emigrated "a rifle gun, ammunition, a blanket, and a brass kettle or a beaver trap." One full blood was quick to point out the hypocrisy in such an offer. "A few years ago," he commented, "The Great Father sent the plow and hoe—said it was not good for his red children to hunt—they must cultivate the earth. Now he tells them there is good hunting in Arkansas; if they will go there he will give them rifles."

It was less than a hundred years since the Cherokees had made their first treaty with the English, and over one-half the lands they once claimed were now gone. Even in the years from 1798 to 1819, when they were diligently walking the road of the white man's civilization, twenty-four separate land cessions had been wrenched from them on a variety of pretenses, many of them in payment for debts run up in Jefferson's factory stores. It was not long before U.S. Commissioners once again came for land. In 1822 they appeared among the tribe, spreading bribes as they went (one of them, for twelve thousand dollars, was contemptuously refused by John Ross). But the Cherokees had been pushed as far as they would go. Any who might have been tempted to sign away the people's birthright remembered the fate of Doublehead. The Cherokees met in council and passed a resolution solemnly expressing their determination "to hold no treaties with any Commissioners . . . being resolved not to dispose of even one foot of ground . . . ."

The two decades after Andrew Jackson's 1817 treaty were a time of unbelievable and at times almost frantic achievement by the Cherokees. They tried desperately to prepare themselves to face the storm they saw gathering on their horizon and to close all avenues by which they might be betrayed. In 1817 another step toward a centralized government was taken when the Council of Chiefs and Warriors representing fifty-four towns met to form a National Committee, naming the twenty-seven-year-old John Ross as its president. The main focus of attention at this time was still the schools: by 1826, there were eighteen of them in Cherokee country, and it was clear that they were meant to serve the dual purpose of bettering the children individually while protecting the tribe as a whole. As one elderly full blood told a classroom of Cherokee children: "Some of you have been in school five years, and some not so long. You have acquired considerable knowledge. By and by you will have more. This gives me great satisfaction. Remember, the whites are near us. . . . Unless you can speak their lanuguage and read

47

and write as they do, they will be able to cheat you and trample on your rights. Be diligent therefore in your studies."

Some of these students went on from the three R's of these rough-hewn log schoolhouses to places of higher learning. The American Board of Commissioners of Foreign Missions had set up schools among the Cherokees in 1816 with the aim of making "the whole tribe English in their language, civilized in their habits, and Christian in their religion." (If this hope hadn't come about as planned, neither had the more ambitious goal the Board had set for itself upon its founding in 1810: to Christianize the whole pagan world in one generation.) In 1818, the Board offered to take some of the more promising students to the mission school it had established in the small agricultural town of Cornwall, Connecticut, to finish their education. Among those chosen was Major Ridge's son, John, a slight but intense young man of delicate health, and his cousin, a young man with sensitive features named Buck Watie. Watie stopped on the way to Cornwall at the home of an aged man who had presided over the Continental Congress years earlier and took enough of a liking to him to adopt his name, Elias Boudinot.

John Ridge and Boudinot studied Cicero and wrote the florid poetry characteristic of those times. Boudinot was the more scholarly of the two, Ridge the more ambitious. One sought to dominate books, the other to dominate men. On a trip back home to visit his father, John Ridge established himself as a future leader, becoming especially popular among the educated mixed bloods.

At Cornwall, Ridge and Boudinot learned to move gracefully in New England's polite society. It was a far different world from the one they had been born into and at first the Cherokees cut a strange figure. Cornwall prided itself most of all on its tolerance and liberality. The two young Indians pierced this pretense before they returned home, however, for while living and studying in New England both fell in love with white women whom they proposed to marry. John Ridge was denounced in the pulpit of one of Cornwall's churches, the minister scandalized that "an *Indian* should go into a civilized community of New England and marry and carry away one of the finest daughters of the land!" Elias Boudinot and his bride were burned in effigy in the Cornwall commons and feared that they might be lynched before swift horses carried them out of town.

But this had blown over by the time these young men and the other Cherokees who had gone north returned home to take up the positions of national leadership for which they had been groomed. When they arrived their people were busily working their farms and developing their institutions. They were also buzzing over something that would have profound consequences for the Cherokees. In 1821 an unlettered Indian who spoke and read no English returned from a sojourn among the Old Settlers in Arkansas, carrying with him a Cherokee alphabet he had spent years perfecting.

Sequoyah was born in a Cherokee village on the Tennessee River in 1773. Years later, when he was at the height of his fame, a white traveler met him and gave this description: "He is of middle stature and of rather slender form. His features are remarkably regular and his face well formed and rather handsome. His eyes are animated, showing a brilliancy of intellect far superior to the ordinary portion of his fellow men." He was painted once by a white artist who showed him holding up a slate with his alphabet on it, dressed in the traditional turban the Cherokees had taken to wearing and smoking one of their white clay pipes.

Sequoyah (whose "white" name was George Guess or

Gist, and whose father may have been a white soldier of fortune) had grown up like any full blood, although the fact that he was lame in one leg made him less active. He gained renown as an excellent silversmith and artist. His plan to develop a Cherokee alphabet evolved gradually; the people remembered him sitting day after day puzzling over the way white men spoke to each other by writing on paper. At first he wondered at the magic they must possess to be able to capture speech on paper. He began his own experiments by scratching symbols on a flat stone with a pin. The work took years ("I thought it would be like catching a wild animal and taming it," he once said of his labor). He worked steadily, often using pokeberry juice for ink and writing with a goose quill on bark. He was not the first to try to get the difficult Cherokee language into written form. Since their arrival in the Nation in the early 1800s, Moravians and other missionaries had tried too; but they and the linguists helping them had failed.

Sequoyah was ridiculed by his friends and even feared as a sorcerer. At night, by the glow of burning pine knots, he sat alone in a small cabin behind his house and worked on his plan. Even those Cherokees who were sympathetic said it couldn't be done. They reminded him of a story the old men told: In the beginning, the gods had given the Indian the book and the white man a bow and arrow; but the white had stolen the book and run away with it, leaving the weapons behind. This was why the Indian would always be a hunter and the white man able to read.

After many false starts, Sequoyah decided that the characters of his alphabet should represent each of the syllables from which Cherokee words were made. He invented eighty-six characters, and then in 1821, he submitted this alphabet to his skeptical countrymen for a public test. With a large crowd looking on, Sequoyah had respected elders of the tribe dictate messages to him which he wrote down and sent by runnner to his son, who was standing some distance away and who immediately read the messages to others standing with him. The people shook their heads and marveled at what they had seen.

The system could be mastered in a matter of days even by those who were illiterate and had not attended the frontier schools scattered throughout the Nation. Soon it was in use in these schools, supplementing or even replacing English. It gave a genuine Cherokee flavor to learning; if Sequoyah had not perfected his invention, it is possible that mainly the sons and daughters of the increasingly prosperous mixed bloods would have had learning and Cherokee culture might have become more imitative of the white man's. But in a year's time, knowledge of Sequoyah's new alphabet had spread through the Nation.

Meanwhile a young minister named Samuel Austin Worcester arrived from the North. He would leave a broad mark on Cherokee history in other ways as well, but he began by setting up a printing press, the type for Sequoyah's alphabet having been especially cast in Boston at the cost of fifteen hundred dollars, one-fourth the Nation's entire governmental budget. Worcester, whom the Indians called "The Messenger," was soon printing the *Cherokee Phoenix*, a bilingual national newspaper edited by Elias Boudinot, a translation of the New Testament into Cherokee, and dozens of other books and pamphlets. As the people saw their language in print just like the white man's, they took heart and worked harder, proud that all this had been inspired by an Indian like them working alone for years in a backwoods cabin.

While news of Sequoyah's invention was spreading

through the Nation, there were other rapid changes taking place in Cherokee country. Samuel Worcester described the tribe in this way when he arrived: "The houses of the Cherokees are of all sorts, from the elegant painted or brick mansion down to a very mean cabin. If one speaks, however, of the mass of the people, they live in comfortable log houses . . . sometimes of hewn logs and sometimes unhewn, commonly with a wooden chimney and a floor of puncheons, or what a New England man would call slabs." The tribal leaders were putting the finishing touches on the government organization they hoped would allow them to face the dark days ahead. They had provided for the election of a Principal Chief who would preside over a bicameral legislature; there were eight circuit judges in the Nation and, in 1822, a Supreme Court was established in the capital town of New Echota (near present-day Calhoun, Georgia).

In 1827, after three weeks of discussion about the wording, the Cherokees adopted a constitution patterned on that of the United States. Its preamble began: "We, the Representatives of the people of the Cherokee Nation, . . . in order to establish justice, ensure tranquility, promote our common welfare, and secure to ourselves and our posterity the blessings of liberty: acknowledging with humility and gratitude the goodness of the sovereign Ruler of the Universe . . . do ordain and establish this constitution for the government of the Cherokee Nation."

The Cherokees chose John Ross to lead them. When he became chief he was thirty-eight years old and was respected by the people. He and Quatie, the full-blood woman he had married, would eventually earn their love as well. Along with men like Major Ridge and his son John, Elias Boudinot and his brother Stand Watie (who had kept the family name), Ross had helped guide the Cherokees the great distance they had come along the white man's path. Boudinot, on a speaking tour of northern cities in 1826 to help raise money to support the *Cherokee Phoenix*, summarized for his audience exactly how far this was. In addition to all the educational, cultural, and governmental achievements, he cited the raw facts of Cherokee national life: 22,000 cattle in the Nation, 7,600 horses, 762 looms, 2,488 spinning wheels, 10 sawmills, 31 gristmills, 62 blacksmith shops. Cherokees had become successful farmers; the land was owned by all the people, with each Indian having the right to clear and cultivate as much land as he wanted, providing that he stayed one-quarter mile from his nearest neighbor. There was so much cotton grown in the Nation, Boudinot pointed out, that after the people had used what they needed there was enough left to export. In less than thirty years, he concluded enthusiastically, the Nation had fulfilled the goals set out by the federal government: it was "civilized."

But in 1828 two events occurred which cast shadows over the Cherokees' jubilation. Gold was discovered on their lands, and Andrew Jackson was elected President of the United States. As Georgians sweating with gold fever stampeded into Indian country, Jackson was making it clear that he would not rest until he had taken every inch of Indian land east of the Mississippi. When he heard of the new President's plans, the aged chief Junaluska let his mind wander back to the days of the Creek War when he had fought alongside the new President. "If I had known that Jackson would drive us from our homes," he was heard to say, "I would have killed him that day on the Horseshoe."

III.
People Die
Very Much

As the Cherokees watched the white expansion that had been stalking them for years draw dangerously close, they desperately marshaled all their energy and resourcefulness for the final battle for their homeland. In an 1829 Council meeting, some of the tribal elders spoke of their persistent worries that the Nation would be betrayed from within; they asked for passage of a formal law making the sale of Cherokee lands without the consent of the people an act of treason punishable by death. The aged chief Womankiller, his gaunt face wrinkled like old parchment, rose to plead for its passage. "My children," he began, looking around at the younger progressives who were taking over leadership of the tribe from his generation. "Permit me to call you so, as I am an old man and have lived a long time, watching the well-being of this Nation .... The bill before you is to punish wicked men .... It is a good law .... My companions in the council who now sleep in the dust spoke the same language, and I now stand on the verge of the grave to bear witness to their love of country. My sun of existence is now fast approaching to the setting, and my aged bones will soon be laid under ground . . . . When I sleep forever, I hope my bones will not be deserted by you."

But laws were as delicate as the old ones' hopes. The Tribal Council knew that it might regulate the Cherokee people, but never the people of Georgia. Ultimately, the Indians' only possible protection was the decency and good faith of the United States and the state of Georgia. But this was to prove the most fragile reed of all.

The frontiersmen who lived side by side with the Cherokees might have learned to get along with them in time. As the civilization program had developed, there had been increasing respect between the red and white men carving a life out of the wilderness. But the land speculators and politicians of Georgia began to whip the Cherokees' neighbors into a frenzy of greed with tales of gold and free land. The fact that it was Indian land only made it more attractive, for this conveyed to the popular imagination (as it still does) the image of virgin forests touched only by the soft track of the moccasin. By the late 1820s people were massing on Cherokee borders. Whites came from all around spurred on by talk of a rush for the only open space left east of the Mississippi. Even the music they hummed was about this land hunger. One popular song began:

"All I want in this creation/
is a pretty little wife and big plantation/
way down yonder in the Cherokee Nation . . . ."

Meanwhile, Georgia stepped up its campaign to drive the Indians out beyond its borders. Like the United States as a whole, the state felt that it too had a manifest destiny.

55

The Cherokees claimed that they constituted a separate Nation, not a part of Georgia, and referred to the solemn treaties by which the white man guaranteed them their lands, in the old language, "for as long as the sun shines and the waters run." But Georgia's Governor Gilmer said cynically, "Treaties were expedients by which ignorant, intractable and savage people were induced without bloodshed to yield up what civilized peoples had a right to possess." He cited the 1802 Compact Thomas Jefferson had made with Georgia and called upon the federal government to carry out its provisions.

But this compact had not been as binding as Georgia claimed. Even Thomas Jefferson had never really contemplated having to enforce it by physically removing Indians, and his successors had agreed. In 1824, President James Monroe had rejected any notion that the federal government had an obligation to uproot the Cherokees. As he wrote, "The Indian title was not affected in the slightest by the compact with Georgia, and there is no obligation on the United States to remove the Indians by force." He pointed out to Georgia's representatives at the time that it was not as if they had received nothing from the agreement: since Jefferson's time, the government had, at a cost of better than $7 million, purchased for the state some twenty-four thousand square miles of land within its borders that had once been claimed by various Indian tribes. But in 1829 Monroe was gone and Andrew Jackson was President. The Cherokees waited nervously to see what their old nemesis would do. There was much talk in Washington about the rights of the common man. Had the old Indian fighter changed his ways in the years since the Creek War? Words were one thing, but did he really want to force them out of their homeland?

In 1829, when Jackson gave his first State of the Union message, the suspense ended. The President's new coonskin democracy was to be based on opening the western states to the constituency of dirt farmers and small shopkeepers who had elected him, men exactly like those in Georgia who now clamored for Indian land. And very high on Jackson's list of priorities was war against the Cherokees—a war to be fought in legislative chambers, not in the backwoods, but an all-out war nonetheless, with no quarter given or accepted. The President told Congress that he was introducing the Indian Removal Act which would uproot all the southeastern tribes, including the Five Civilized Tribes, and move them across the Mississippi to the *terra incognita* then called Indian Territory. Eleven days after this announcement, with the Indians still in a state of shock over the news, Georgia, reassured that the federal government would not hinder it, passed a series of appalling laws—The Indian Codes—intended to paralyze the Cherokees' national life and make their existence in Georgia intolerable.

These Indian Codes anticipated the infamous Black Codes of the post-Civil War period by which the South returned the emancipated slaves to the less formal bondage of Jim Crow. The difference was that in 1830 Georgia was concerned with the Indians' land, not their persons. Without warning, its legislature provided for the confiscation of large sections of Cherokee country; made the Cherokee Nation's laws null and void; prohibited any Indian from testifying in court against a white man; and provided for the imprisonment of any Indian who spoke against emigration across the Mississippi. The Nation's recently discovered gold fields were also confiscated, and the Codes forbade any Indian from extracting precious metals from Georgia soil. Finally, all Cherokee lands were to be surveyed and mapped out into homestead lots of 160 acres and "gold lots" of 40 acres, to be distributed to Georgia citizens by a public lottery.

While the Codes brought a reign of terror down on the Cherokee Nation, President Jackson and federal officials sat back, watching the chaos develop. Bands of mounted vigilantes called "Pony Clubs" (foreshadowing the Ku Klux Klan of later days) invaded Cherokee lands, killing livestock, setting fires, and committing occasional murders. All the rules of decency which whites had been urging Cherokees to learn for some forty years were now ignored. In one notorious case two whites who had been invited to dinner by a wealthy Cherokee mixed blood took advantage of his absence later on in the evening to drive his children and their nurse out of the house, which they then looted and set on fire. The men were eventually brought to trial, but the case against them was dismissed because of the new rule that Indians could not testify against whites in the courtroom. A people who had governed themselves justly and peaceably for generations watched helplessly as disorder spread like a disease through their lands.

Time and again, the Cherokees sent John Ross and other leaders to appeal for relief from these outrages. But Andrew Jackson, who had known in advance of Georgia's intentions, told them: "The President of the United States has no power to protect you against the laws of Georgia." He sent a small contingent of federal troops to the troubled area, but it was to "keep order" in the gold fields, where white miners worried that the Indians would finally pick up weapons to defend themselves while retaking their confiscated territory. The Cherokees realized that the President of the United States was no less determined to break the backbone of their resistance than was Georgia.

Writing in the *Cherokee Phoenix*, Elias Boudinot warned his people: "This is the circumstance we have for a long time dreaded . . . . It has been the desire of our enemies that the Cherokees may be urged to some desperate act. Thus far this desire has never been realized, and we hope, notwithstanding the great injury now sustained, this forbearance will continue." The Cherokees followed his advice and determined to stand fast despite the violence committed against them.

Meanwhile Jackson escalated his war by cutting off the six-thousand-dollar annuity paid for decades by previous Presidents into the Cherokees' national treasury. This money was payment for the hundreds of thousands of acres of Indian land taken in the past, and the Cherokees had used it to fund their schools and their national newspaper. The President also resorted to bribery, which he had used effectively in his negotiations with Indians after the Creek War and more recently in his dealings with the Choctaw Nation, whose chiefs had been paid to betray their people in 1830 by signing the Treaty of Dancing Rabbit Creek which obliged them to move beyond the Mississippi. Now Jackson's agents secretly employed James Rogers, an influential Cherokee mixed blood, to obtain his people's agreement to removal. The unsuccessful Rogers admitted later on that he had been offered "a liberal reward which would place myself and family in easy circumstances the balance of my life."

The conspiracy between federal and state governments poisoned the atmosphere of the Nation, and fear walked hand in hand with disorder. Late in 1831, when John Ross was riding to a town meeting to talk to his people about their predicament, a Georgian jumped out of ambush and yelled, "Ross, I've wanted to kill you for a long time, and I'm damned if I don't do it now." He leveled his rifle, but it misfired, and before he could reload, the Cherokee Chief spurred his horse and managed to escape.

The intimidation the Cherokees faced was also aimed at

the other Five Civilized Tribes, and by 1832, the Chickasaws
and Creeks had joined the Choctaws in signing treaties agree-
ing to removal. The Seminoles had retreated in arms to the
Everglades where the Americans later followed them and
spent $20 million and 1,500 of their own soldiers' lives in an
extended war. During this time the Cherokees held their
ground peacefully but stubbornly. All the bribes, threats,
and promises of U.S. Indian agents managed to convince
only 626 of their people to emigrate voluntarily. The Nation
made no secret of its defiance. Cherokee leaders proudly
compared their situation to an open space where a tornado
has struck, knocking over everything but one proud tree
which continues to stand. The volatile John Ridge, who
joined his father, John Ross, and Elias Boudinot in constant
pilgrimages to Washington seeking Congressional support,
scornfully called Andrew Jackson a "Chicken Snake who
comes to crawl and hide in the luxuriant grass of his nefari-
ous hypocrisy." The National Council met—illegally now
—and put aside its dreams of establishing a national
museum, library, and university. Even if there had
been time for these pursuits, there was no money. The
Cherokee treasury was empty, but in the first nine months
of 1830 over $250,000 mined from their gold fields had been
received in Augusta alone, and a mint in the town of Gains-
ville was stamping $100 a day in gold coin.

The struggle was simply for survival, and the Council
drafted a resolution to the President. "Inclination to remove
from this land has no abiding place in our hearts," it read,
"and when we move we shall move only by the course of
nature to sleep under the ground which the great spirit gave
to our ancestors . . . ." When Jackson ignored them, they
appealed directly to the American people in a petition written
July 17, 1830: "We wish to remain on the land of our fathers.

We have a perfect and original right to remain without interruption or molestation. The treaties with us, and the laws of the United States made in persuance of treaties, guarantee our residence and our privilege and secure us against intruders. Our only request is that these treaties may be fulfilled and these laws executed . . . . It is under a sense of the most pungent feelings that we make this, perhaps our last appeal to the good people of the United States." John Ross himself warned that "possessions acquired by unjust and unrighteous means will sooner or later prove a curse to those who sought them, we have been taught by that holy religion brought to us by the white man . . . . We would with Christian sympathy avert the wrath of Heaven from the United States by imploring your government to be just."

The brutal treatment of the Cherokees soon became a cause célèbre for the whole nation, a moral crisis that would be eclipsed later only by the question of slavery. Georgia and other Southern states may have been united against the Indian, but there was sympathy in the North. Close to half the members of the U.S. Senate publicly supported the Cherokee Nation, and when Elias Boudinot and John Ridge went on fund-raising tours to cities like Philadelphia, they spoke to jammed auditoriums where the listeners gave liberal sums to aid their fight. Soon the predicament of this unique tribe of Indians became a constitutional crisis as well as a moral one, when a group of Northern lawyers volunteered to take its case to the highest tribunals in the land.

In March 1831, the case of *The Cherokee Nation* v. *Georgia* was heard before the Supreme Court. The Cherokees' attorneys argued that the tribe constituted a separate and sovereign nation and that neither the federal nor state government had the right to impose its laws upon them. But in its

61

landmark decision the Court decided that it had no jurisdiction over this matter because—as Chief Justice John
Marshall said at the time—"an Indian tribe or nation within
the United States is not a foreign nation in the sense of the
constitution . . . ."

It was a setback, but there was still hope: two of the
justices had dissented from this majority opinion (which
had at least admitted that the Cherokees were indeed a
nation, "a domestic, dependent nation under the protection
of the federal government") and the Chief Justice himself
was known to be sympathetic to their cause. (Fiercely opposed to Jackson and his policies, Marshall had once written
of Indians: "Every oppression now exercised on a helpless
people depending on our magnanimity and justice for the
preservation of their existence impresses a deep stain on the
American character.") The Cherokees' attorneys waited for
a better case to bring before the Court. The occasion was not
long in coming.

Georgia had long since decided that these Indians,
whom they still believed were savages, were racially so inferior that they were not capable of waging by themselves
a spirited and intelligent fight against removal. The key to
their resistance had to be the handful of white missionaries
who had lived among the Nation since the early 1800s. With
this in mind, the Georgia legislature moved quickly to pass
another law. It forbade any white man from residing among
the Cherokees unless he had taken an oath of allegiance to
the laws of the state. Despite their troubled consciences, most
of the missionaries signed this oath. But Samuel Austin
Worcester, who had come to Georgia to help set up the
Cherokee Phoenix, did not. To do so, he said, was to support
the Indian Codes. After repeatedly refusing to sign the oath,

Worcester was finally dragged from his home by a company of Georgia militiamen, arrested, and jailed. He was tried and sentenced to four years at hard labor. After his trial, Worcester was offered one more chance to sign. But again he refused, and the doors of prison closed upon him.

On March 4, 1832, the Cherokees' lawyers brought the case of *Samuel A. Worcester* v. *The State of Georgia* before the Supreme Court. This time John Marshall and the majority ruled that the law by which the missionary was imprisoned was unconstitutional. They went on to say that only the federal government, not Georgia, had jurisdiction over the tribe. "The Cherokee Nation," the momentous decision read, "is a distinct community, occupying its own territory . . . in which the laws of Georgia can have no right to enter but with the consent of the Cherokees."

There was dancing, feasting, and celebration when news of the decision reached the Indians. It meant that the infamous Indian Codes were unconstitutional and that Georgians were trespassing on Cherokee lands. Elias Boudinot, who was on a Northern speaking tour, wrote home exuberantly to his brother Stand Watie: "The laws of the state are declared by the highest judicial tribunal in the country to be null and void . . . . The question is forever settled as to who is right and who is wrong."

But right and wrong, the Indian soon came to realize, had nothing to do with their dilemma. Soon it became clear that Georgia authorities were going to defy the Supreme Court. (They kept Worcester in jail another year before finally releasing him.) And Andrew Jackson's scorn for the decision and the Court itself was clear in the famous remark: "John Marshall has rendered his decision; now let him enforce it." Soon there were more than five hundred surveyors on Cherokee lands cutting them up into segments for the public lottery. Whatever the Supreme Court said, there would be no relief for the Indians.

It has been said that President Jackson acted as he did because he feared enforcement of the Supreme Court decision would lead to war with Georgia and an end to the Union. But in 1832 he had indicated a willingness to send troops to South Carolina to enforce the federally imposed tariff, even though that state had murmured angrily about seceding from the Union. Jackson ignored the Supreme Court's decision simply because he wanted the Cherokees on their way across the Mississippi.

John Marshall and others feared that the Constitution would be destroyed by Jackson's failure to uphold and enforce the Supreme Court decision. But they were wrong. It was not long before the constitutional crisis passed, along with all the moral fervor it had aroused. After all the bitter words were over, both the supreme law of the land and the Union were still standing, undiminished in strength. Only the Indians had lost.

Georgia's lottery for Cherokee lands was completed by 1833, a delay having been caused when it was discovered that the officials in charge had rigged the process to allow their friends and relatives to draw choice lots. Soon the settlers began to pour into Cherokee territory. Like locusts, they devoured everything in their path. They dispossessed Indians of elegant homes and rough cabins alike. When John Ross returned from one of his innumerable and frustrating trips to Washington, he found his home had been confiscated by a white man. He was forced to move his family to a one-room shack just over the border in Tennessee.

Most of the Indians calmly moved back into the hills

or into other states beyond Georgia's jurisdiction. It was humiliating, but it could be borne. John Ross saddled his old gray horse and went from one settlement to another, listening to the people and telling them to be patient, continue to stay where they were, pray for justice, and wait for better times.

But other Cherokee leaders had second thoughts about further resistance. Cautiously, almost inaudibly, there was whispered talk of coming to terms with Jackson. What soon exploded into a bitter factional split that would haunt the tribe for the next thirty years began as doubts on the part of John Ridge, old Major Ridge, Elias Boudinot, and a few others. All of them had for a time been in the forefront of the fight against removal; all were patriots. But the flamboyant John Ridge, whose wit and eloquence had made him popular with the educated mixed bloods in the tribe even while he was still a student at Cornwall, chafed especially under the steady hand of John Ross. He aspired to be Principal Chief himself. But Ridge did not turn against the Nation's policies simply because his personal ambition was blocked. Like the others in what became known as the Treaty Party, he really believed that further resistance was useless and would only narrow the Indians' already restricted range of choice. At first in secret and then openly, late in 1832, this group favored compromise. Ross begged them not to weaken the Nation by breaking ranks. "Our country and our people," he wrote to John Ridge in 1834, "should always be our motto and their will should direct us in the path of duty." The people too made it clear that they did not want any treaty that meant giving up their homeland. But John Ridge said that the Cherokees had been misguided and must now bow to the inevitable. When the Council disagreed with their plans, the Treaty Party accused John Ross of manipulating the full bloods simply to increase his personal power. Finally John Ridge and the others resolved to act on their own.

Putting their own view of the problem facing the tribe above the people's wishes was the Treaty Party's critical error. Whatever his private feelings, John Ross knew that the Cherokee people had their own ideas and that the job of a leader was simply to serve their wishes. If he hadn't done this, he would not have been their Chief for over thirty years. Samuel Worcester, who developed a deep personal friendship for Elias Boudinot after working closely with him on the *Cherokee Phoenix*, admitted as much in a letter sent back home to Connecticut. "Nothing is plainer than that it is the earnest wish of the whole body of people to remain where they are," he wrote. "If there were a chief in favor of removal he would be overawed by the people." The other missionaries echoed his sentiments in a petition supporting the Cherokees. "There is overwhelming evidence," they said, "that no man—whatever degree of talent or knowledge or previous influence—could possibly find his way into office at the present time whose views were against those of the mass of the people on the grand subject of national interest —removal to the west."

But the Treaty Party went its own way, convinced of the righteousness of its cause. As it did so, it became more and more alienated from the people. The Ridges and Boudinot soon found themselves accepting special consideration from Georgia officials, who saw them as the Trojan Horse that could be sent into the heart of the Cherokee Nation. First, the property of members of the Treaty Party was temporarily exempted from the lottery. Then Georgia's new Governor Wilson Lumpkin told one of his agents to "assure Boudinot, Ridge and their friends of state protection under any circumstances. I shall feel it my imperative duty to afford them every security . . . ." When the Treaty Party went to Washington to negotiate with President Jackson in competition with John Ross and against the will of the people, they were given three thousand dollars in traveling money by the state.

Now that the united front had broken, Georgia intensified its pressure. Early in 1835, the *Phoenix*, which had been one of the main weapons in the Cherokees' struggle, was confiscated. John Ross was arrested on a fabricated charge by Georgia militiamen and sat for thirteen days in a backwoods jail, the decaying corpse of a Cherokee hanged days before suspended above him from the prison rafters. Then in March a secret treaty was drawn up without the knowledge of the people by the Ridges and a handful of other Cherokee leaders. It provided for the cession of all the Nation's lands east of the Mississippi in return for $3,250,000 (later raised to $5,000,000) and lands in Indian territory.

When the people heard what had happened, they were outraged. Once more they had been betrayed from within. There was talk of killing John Ridge, Boudinot, and others who had drawn up what the full bloods called "the dirty paper." But Ross steered the Nation away from internal violence. Once more he wearily journeyed to Washington after a council meeting in October attended by thousands of Cherokees who had almost unanimously shouted no when asked if they approved of the proposed treaty. But events were moving fast. Whatever it took, Jackson was determined to force the removal of these stubborn Indians. Government agents had called a meeting in the capital town of New Echota to explain the treaty once again to the Cherokees and obtain their agreement once and for all. Circulars were distributed through all the towns in the Nation informing

the people of the meeting and warning that any who boycotted it would be counted as voting in favor of the treaty.
But John Ross and the other anti-treaty leaders stayed away,
and in the end barely three hundred Indians were there on
that bleak morning of December 21, 1835.

One of them was Major Ridge. He looked grim and
depressed. Probably better than anyone else present, he knew
the magnitude of the act that was taking place. Perhaps he
thought back on the day over twenty-five years earlier when
he had executed the traitor Doublehead for selling the Nation's lands against the people's will. Much had happened
since then. When it came time, he stood up to tell the
Cherokees why he supported this agreement. "We obtained
the land from the living God," he said, trying to hold back
the tears that rimmed his eyes. "The Georgians got their
title from the British. Yet they are strong and we are weak.
We are few, they are many . . . . We can never forget these
homes, I know, but an unbending, iron necessity tells us
we must leave them. I would willingly die to preserve them,
but any forcible effort to keep them will cost us our lives
and the lives of our children. There is but one path of
safety . . . . Give up these lands and go over beyond the
Great Father of Waters."

The next week, on the evening of December 29, the
members of the Treaty Party gathered at the elegant home
of Elias Boudinot. Huddled around the parlor table in the
candlelight, they came forward one by one to sign the
treaty. As Major Ridge made his mark on the paper, he
was heard to murmur under his breath, "I have signed my
death warrant."

Even though all but a small minority of the tribe had
rejected it, the Treaty of New Echota went on to the U.S.
Senate for ratification. Nearly sixteen thousand Cherokees—

almost the whole tribe—signed a petition denouncing it as a fraud, naively believing that this near unanimous evidence of their feelings would have an effect; rallies protesting the treaty as a national dishonor were held in many Northern cities; and legislators as different as New England's Daniel Webster and Tennessee's Davy Crockett rose to speak against it in Congress. But Andrew Jackson backed it with all the power of his office, and the Senate passed it by a single fateful vote. Cherokee removal was set for 1838, two years away. Georgia's Governor Wilson Lumpkin wrote Andrew Jackson a long, reassuring letter. "The statements of Ross and others that the late treaty was made contrary to the will of the people," he said, "is entitled to no respect or consideration whatever. Nineteen-twentieths of the Cherokees are too ignorant and depraved to entitle their opinions to any weight or consideration in such matters."

Ralph Waldo Emerson, philosopher laureate of the nation, wrote an impassioned open letter to the President which echoed the helpless outrage much of the country felt about the injustice about to be visited on the Cherokees: "Sir, does this government think that the people of the United States are become savage and mad? From their mind are the sentiments of love and a good nature wiped clean out? The soul of man, the justice, the mercy that is the heart's heart in all men, from Maine to Georgia, does abhor this business . . . . A crime is projected that confounds our understandings by its magnitude, a crime that really deprives us as well as the Cherokees of a country, for how could we call the conspiracy that should crush these poor Indians our government, or the land that was cursed by their parting . . . our country any more?"

But this plea was ignored. (Southerners were quick to point out that the North could afford to oppose removal since it had annihilated the Indians in its area a century earlier.) The day belonged to men like Andrew Jackson and Governor Lumpkin, who noted cynically: "Paper may be filled with . . . wailing over the departure of the Cherokees from the bones of their forefathers. But if the heads of these pretended mourners were waters, and their eyes were a fountain of tears, and they were to spend days and years in weeping over the departure of the Cherokees from Georgia, yet they will go!"

General John Ellis Wool, who had been placed in command of federal troops stationed in Georgia to explain the treaty to the Indians and prevent any opposition to it, found his job distasteful. "It is vain to talk to a people almost universally opposed to the treaty," he wrote home to his family. "Many have said they will die before they will leave the country." He added that even desolate, hungry Cherokees pathetically refused gifts of blankets and food the Army offered, because they were afraid that accepting them would compromise their cause. General R. G. Dunlap, in charge of a company of Tennessee volunteers also on the scene, threatened to resign because he felt his state dishonored "by aiding . . . at the point of a bayonet a treaty against the will and authority of the Cherokee people."

But even though their laws had been abolished, their lands overrun, their schools closed, their interests betrayed, and their precious unity broken, the Cherokees still tried to remain firm. John Ross maneuvered in every way he could think of, traveling back and forth from Washington where he hoped to persuade the new President Martin Van Buren to reconsider Jackson's policy toward the Nation. Ross attempted to rally Cherokee supporters in the Senate to overturn the Treaty of New Echota legally or to find some other way of allowing his people to retain even a small portion of their land.

But on March 27, 1838, Congress refused once and for all to grant relief to the Cherokees. Time, which had been as much an enemy of the Indians as Andrew Jackson, had finally run out. Only two thousand Indians had removed voluntarily (among them the Ridges, Boudinot, and others in the Treaty Party), and in May 1838, General Winfield Scott arrived in the Nation with seven thousand troops— almost one soldier for every two Indians—to remove the rest of the Cherokee Nation by force. The great tragedy now entered its final act.

In the 1880s, an anthropologist named James Mooney lived with the Cherokees and studied the remnants of their legends and sacred beliefs. He found that many of the old men and women still remembered the terrible times of removal; after listening to their stories, he painstakingly recreated what it had been like. "Under Scott's orders," he wrote, "the troops were disposed at various points through the Cherokee country, where stockade forts were erected for gathering in and holding the Indians preparatory to removal. Squads of troops were sent to search out with rifle and bayonet every small cabin hidden away in the coves or by the sides of mountain streams, to seize and bring in as prisoners all the occupants, however or wherever they might be found. Families at dinner were startled by the sudden gleam of bayonets in the doorway and rose up to be driven with blows and oaths along the weary miles of trail that led to the stockade. Men were seized in their fields or going along the road, women were taken from their wheels and children from their play. In many cases, on turning for one last look, they saw their homes in flames, fired by the lawless rabble that followed on the heels of the soldiers to loot and pillage. Systematic hunts were made by the same men for Indians' graves, to rob them of the silver pendants and other valuables deposited with the dead . . . . To prevent escape, soldiers had been ordered to approach and surround each house and come upon the occupants without warning. One old patriarch, when thus surprised, calmly called his children and grandchildren around him, and kneeling down, bid them pray with him in their own language. Then rising, he led the way into exile."

For every Indian rounded up there was a tragic story. Two children ran into the woods to escape the soldiers. Their mother begged to be allowed to go and find them, promising that she would then come to the stockade voluntarily, but she was driven off with the other prisoners. Families were separated, never to see each other again; in one instance, a confused deaf mute who turned right when ordered to go left was shot and killed for his error. A Colonel Ziles, then an officer in the Georgia militia who took part in the round-up, wrote of it several years later, "I fought through the Civil War and I have seen men shot to pieces and slaughtered by the thousands, but the Cherokee removal was the cruelest work I ever knew."

Several hundred Indians managed to elude the soldiers and escape to the hills. They lived in caves and subsisted on roots and berries and whatever else they could forage. One of them, Tsali, became a legendary figure and a symbol of Cherokee bravery during these terrible times. Not much is known about him, but it is said that he escaped to the hills after killing a soldier who had menaced his wife with a bayonet. Army authorities knew it would be difficult to catch these Cherokees, so they offered a bargain: if Tsali would give himself up, the others would be allowed to stay while the government decided what to do with them.[1] Hearing of the proposal, Tsali surrendered so that the people would not be hunted down.

On a soft summer morning he faced the firing squad. When the young officer in charge walked up and scornfully asked if he had any last words, Tsali took a long look around him and said simply, "It is sweet to die in one's country." Then he buckled to his knees as the volley of gunfire rang out. The U.S. Army had forced weeping Cherokee prisoners to act as his executioners.

John Ross had stayed in Washington, pleading with legislators, in the hope that he would somehow be able to save his people from their terrible ordeal. When he saw that he could no longer ask for a reconsideration of the treaty, he tried to get permission for sick and aged Indians to live out their days in their homeland and negotiated successfully for the release of all Cherokees imprisoned in Georgia jails. When he returned home in 1838, he found even more work: his people were penned up like cattle in filthy, disease-ridden stockades which had been hurriedly constructed to receive them. Hundreds had already died in these camps; and the first detachments of Cherokees sent west under Army escort had been decimated by fevers and other illnesses. After meeting with the remnants of the National Council, Ross went to General Scott and asked that the Cherokees be allowed to supervise their own removal in the fall, after the

---

[1] They would eventually be allowed to stay after years of negotiation. Today they live on the Qualla reservation in North Carolina, their numbers having grown over the years to around five thousand.

73

season of sickness had passed. To the annoyance of Andrew Jackson, in retirement at his Hermitage, the request was granted.

In October, the exiles readied for their final leave-taking. Some left behind beautifully furnished brick homes with calf-bound books in the libraries and blooded racehorses in the paddock; most left only a small cabin, some farming tools, perhaps a few farm animals. Their common loss was what all cherished most: the land where the Cherokee people had lived since time out of mind, where their ancestors lay buried, and where their Nation had been born, flourished beyond anyone's expectations, and resisted the might of the U.S. government in every way it knew how. They stopped at a place in Tennessee south of the Hiwassee River to hold a final council. After pledging to continue their old laws and constitution in their new home in Indian Territory, the Cherokees left in groups on the forced march west.

Some of the contingents went by keelboat on the Mississippi and Arkansas rivers; most went overland, walking hundreds of miles through Georgia, Tennessee, Kentucky, Missouri, and Arkansas, and finally arriving in the vast land known as Indian Territory. Hungry and threadbare, they hunched forward into the winter winds and struggled across snow drifts with only cloth wrappings on their bare and bleeding feet. Each new dawn brought more deaths. A traveler from Maine reported seeing a Cherokee woman carrying a sick baby in her arms. "All she could do was make it as comfortable as circumstances would permit," he wrote home in shock. "She could only carry her dying child in her arms a few miles further and then she must stop in a strange land and consign her baby to the cold ground and then pass on with the multitude." A beloved old

74

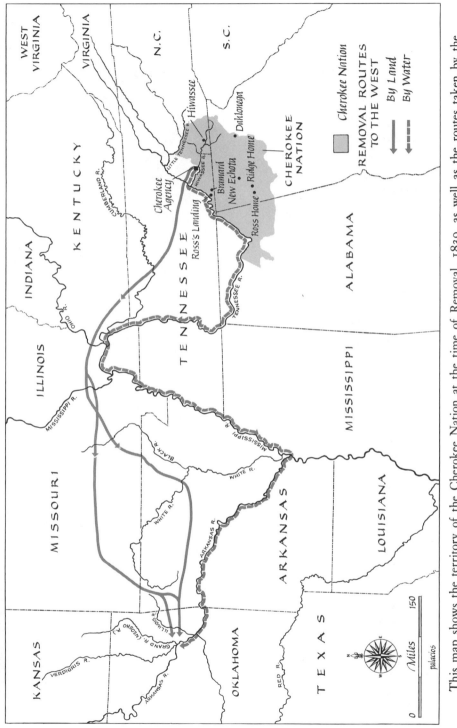

This map shows the territory of the Cherokee Nation at the time of Removal, 1839, as well as the routes taken by the Cherokees during removal to Indian Territory. Present-day names and boundaries of states have been used.

chief, Whitepath, was another who died along the way. His party stopped long enough to bury him, marking the grave with a tall pole flying a pennant of white linen so that the groups who followed would know that an honored man lay at the side of the road.

The route they traveled was known forever after as the Trail of Tears—in Cherokee, *Nunna-da-ul-tsun-yi,* The Place Where They Cried. A white observer in the area wrote to friends of what he had seen: "The sick and feeble were carried in wagons . . . a great many ride on horseback and multitudes go on foot. Even aged women, apparently nearly ready to drop into the grave, were travelling with heavy burdens attached to their back—on sometimes frozen ground and sometimes muddy streets, with no covering for the feet . . . . We learned from the inhabitants on the road where the Indians passed that they buried fourteen or fifteen at every stopping place . . . ."

John Ross oversaw the packing of all Cherokee records: the letters from Presidents since George Washington, the Nation's first written laws, all the broken and dishonored treaties. Then he too set out with his family. Along the way, his wife Quatie fell sick with a fever. But when they came upon a party of fullbloods she noticed that one of the children was ill and she got down off their wagon to give him her blanket. Shortly afterward, her fever grew worse. She caught pneumonia. Like others, she died and was buried in a shallow grave.

By early 1839, the last of the stragglers had reached their new home in the West. For weeks the people watched in hopes that there would be others. But they didn't come. More than four thousand Cherokees had died, almost a quarter of those who set out. The people were stunned. They could not believe what had happened to them. One old full blood later recalled these terrible times in broken English that hints at the extent of the tragedy. "Long time we travel on way to new land," he said. "People feel bad when they leave old Nation. Womens cry and make sad wails. Children cry and many men cry and all look sad like when friends die. But they say nothing and just put heads down and keep on go towards West. Many days pass and people die very much."

IV.
A Far Distant Country

During the first days after the gaunt and fevered emigrants had arrived in Indian Territory, the Cherokee Nation was in a state of shock. As it counted its losses, the tribe tried desperately to recover its sense of balance and direction. The people had been torn from the rivers and mountains which had been the center of their life for hundreds of years; their council fires had been put out and their houses burned behind them. As the anthropologist James Mooney wrote years later, "They were transported bodily to a far distant country where everything was new and strange . . . ."

This new place was not like the homeland where the tribe had lived for centuries, but it wasn't barren either. John Ridge had written enthusiastically of the Honey Creek area in the northern part of the Cherokees' new lands (in present-day Oklahoma) where he had decided to settle: "Never did I see a better location for settlements and better springs in the world. God has thrown his favors here with a broad cast." But the major problem the Cherokees faced didn't have anything to do with the fertility of their new soil; it was whether or not the deep wounds in their unity as a tribe could ever be healed. Before the Cherokees could face the future squarely, an epilogue to the tragedy started in Georgia had to be played out.

It began just after dawn on the morning of June 22, 1839—six months after the last weary contingent of Indians had arrived in Indian Territory. Already the ground was starting to heat up, and it promised to be another sweltering day at Honey Creek. The morning air was heavy and humid, and only a slight breeze rustled the snowy blooms of the dogwood trees. John Ridge and his family were still sleeping when a group a twenty-five armed Cherokees quietly dismounted from their horses and quickly surrounded the newly built log house. Their faces set in grim lines, three of the Indians nodded at the others and moved forward. They entered the house and returned a moment later dragging the terrified and uncomprehending Ridge by his nightshirt. The group stared down at him in silence for a long moment, and his eyes moved quickly from one face to another looking for a sign of mercy. Then the quiet was pierced by shrill war cries with Ridge's screams rising in a crescendo above them as the men rushed up and drove their knives into his body. While he lay bleeding to death on the ground, each of the Cherokees walked by and ritualistically stepped on his body. Then they mounted their horses and rode off. The day of reckoning had begun.

While John Ridge was being executed at Honey Creek, a second band of Cherokees was making its way to Park Hill, not far from the new capital city of Tahlequah. (A few years later Park Hill became the cultural center of the Nation, a

79

place where Cherokee ladies carried parasols on their strolls through the gardens of fine homes and played Mozart on their parlor pianos.)

Elias Boudinot had been staying here with his friend Samuel Worcester while his own house was being constructed on a nearby knoll. The scholarly Cherokee and the missionary printer had become inseparable working together years earlier on the *Cherokee Phoenix*, and they planned on living close together so they could continue translating Biblical material into Cherokee.

At nine o'clock, Boudinot had just finished breakfast. He said good-by to his wife and left Worcester's back door to walk over and see if the carpenters he had hired were following his instructions. Two Cherokees he had never met before intercepted him on his way. "Can you come with us?" one of them asked. "We have a friend who is sick and needs help." Boudinot, who had some knowledge of medicine, said yes and allowed them to escort him off on a side path. But just as he began to understand what was happening, one of the men drew a knife and stabbed him in the side. As Boudinot sank to his knees, others emerged from hiding places. The morning sun glinted off the hatchets as they flashed down time and again deep into his skull.

Not knowing that his son and cousin Boudinot were already dead, Major Ridge had decided to get up early that morning and pay a visit to a friend. By ten o'clock, he had already been riding for a long time. Just after crossing the Arkansas border, he may have realized that the trail ahead was unusually quiet, but he did not see the Cherokees hidden in the undergrowth ahead. There was an explosion of gunfire, and he was hit five times in the head and body. Man Who Walks on Mountain Tops, as he had been called in the days when he took white scalps, fell from his saddle, dead. The vengeance was complete.

Stand Watie came to claim his brother Elias Boudinot's body later that day. He pulled the sheet back and looked down at the gashed and mutilated face for a moment and then offered a ten-thousand-dollar reward for information about the killers. Though rumors swirled like dust storms through Cherokee settlements, the executioners were never revealed. Watie and others of the Treaty Party knew that they too had been marked for death, and had escaped only by luck or accident.

Outrage over the expulsion from their homeland, pent up for several years, had finally exploded. But this violence was planned without the knowledge of the tribe's leaders. A few days earlier, a group of full bloods from each of the old clans had met in secret. They had ritually read aloud the 1829 law, supported at that time by the Ridges, making the unauthorized sale of Cherokee lands an act punishable by death. Then they had stood in the dimly lit cabin and solemnly drawn lots to see who would carry out the delayed justice. One of them was assigned to stay with John Ross and keep him from finding out about their plan. It was the Blood Law of olden times, a ritual punishment for the most serious crime a Cherokee could commit.

John Ridge had helped make the Treaty of New Echota and had seen it ratified. Just before leaving the old country, however, he had experienced a fleeting moment of doubt. He wrote in his diary: "In the history of the Nation, if there is a page assigned to my name and that of our house, I know not what will be said." If he could have seen a few months into the future, he probably would have acted differently.

Though these executions were a delayed reaction to the Trail of Tears, they were also caused by new frustrations that had been plaguing the Cherokees since their arrival in Indian Territory. The dissension and factionalism that had made the Nation vulnerable to the conspiracy between Andrew Jackson and the state of Georgia had preceded them into the new land. The people wanted to begin sifting through the wreckage of their national life and rebuilding their institutions, but there were many obstacles in their way.

Before the fourteen thousand Cherokees who made the long march out of Georgia commenced their ordeal, four thousand of their kinsmen were already established in Indian Territory. The Ridges and the rest of the Treaty Party had come there shortly after the negotiation of the Treaty of New Echota. But there was also a larger group known as the "Old Settlers"—Cherokees who had fled the white man over the years by migrating westward in a small but steady stream. This migration had begun at the turn of the century when some of Dragging Canoe's Chickamaugans had left the Cherokee Nation rather than adopt the white man's ways. At first the Old Settlers had built homes on lands set aside for them in what became the state of Arkansas. But by 1828, this land too had been invaded by convoys of covered wagons and the Old Settlers were forced by the government to move onto Indian Territory. Those among them who hoped to find a final refuge from the white man soon saw that it was an impossible dream. In their new home they not only skirmished with tribes like the Osages, who had also been forced south from Kansas to Indian Territory, but they saw frontiersmen all around them throwing up shacks and slaughtering the southern herds of buffalo for their tallow as they later would kill the plains herds for their hides. Most ominous of all, there were even whites squatting on lands to the *west* of them. The ring was closing around the Indians.

On arriving in the new land, John Ross and his emigrants faced the animosity of the Old Settlers who had become used to their separate government. As always, the Principal Chief appealed for unity in a large assembly of all factions of the tribe. "Friends," he began in his Victorian style, "through the mysterious dispensation of Providence, we have been permitted to meet in general council on the border of the great plains of the west . . . . We cannot lose sight of the fact that we are all of the household of the Cherokee family and of one blood . . . . Let us kindle our social fire and take measures for cementing our reunion as a Nation." But his call was ignored. The Old Settlers had aligned themselves with the Treaty Party; even before news of the death of the Ridges and Boudinot shot like lightning through Indian Territory, there were fears that it would now take a civil war to settle the differences separating the tribe. Although Ross had known nothing of the executions —and had in fact used his authority to keep the Treaty Party unharmed back in Georgia when many Cherokees wanted to kill them for making the Treaty of New Echota—there were rumors that his life would now be taken by Stand Watie and his men. At one point, over five hundred armed supporters of Ross appeared spontaneously at his new home at Park Hill to stand guard over their leader night and day. Their fears were not groundless. Even General Matthew Arbuckle, military commander of the garrison at nearby Fort Gibson, had hopes that the Principal Chief, by now known nationally as a painful thorn in the side of U.S. Indian policy, would be killed. When one of those who had come to watch over Ross, a man named Charles Coody, saw Arbuckle a few weeks later, the general angrily reproached him: "You too! You shouldered a rifle and went with the rest to guard John Ross. But for that, Ross would have been killed."

Only one leader among the Old Settlers offered support for Ross and his hopes for a reunified Nation, and that was the famous Sequoyah who had been living quietly on a small ten-acre farm among the Old Settlers since 1829. He spent his days riding patiently through small towns teaching the Cherokee alphabet in informal classes. Calling the people together, he would kneel down on the ground, take a charred stick from the fire, and write the letters he had perfected on a piece of smooth bark. He also taught Indian youngsters the lore of The Real People. In the years since his invention, word of Sequoyah and his remarkable accomplishment had spread all over the United States. He may have guessed at the extent of his fame, but if so, he shrugged it off, preferring to remain what he had always been and reacting with embarrassment when whites came to pay homage to him.

Sequoyah attended the July 1839 convention at Park Hill called by Ross and sent a message to the headmen of the Old Settlers who had boycotted the meeting even though many of their people had not: "We are here in council with the late emigrants, and we want you to come up without delay, that we may talk matters over like friends and brothers .... we have no doubt but we can have things amicably and satisfactorily settled." At this meeting an Act of Union was adopted by which the two factions were declared, in the words of John Ross, "one body politic under the style and title of the Cherokee Nation." The old constitution and laws were reaffirmed, Sequoyah signing for the Old Settlers and Ross for the new ones.

Things might have gone smoothly over the next few years, but they didn't. The passions aroused by removal and by the executions of the Ridges could not be easily soothed. As heir of the Treaty Party leadership, Stand Watie defied Ross. He was encouraged to do so by General Arbuckle, the symbol of federal government in the Territory, who saw that the Cherokees could be more easily manipulated if split by factionalism. To create even more dissension, Arbuckle spread the rumor that Ross was getting wealthy while the emigrants—who were due money and goods from the government under provisions of the New Echota Treaty —were paid only sporadically. They would have starved in those early days if it had not been for the generosity of the Old Settlers who set aside factional differences when it came down to questions of hunger and shelter.

Major E. A. Hitchcock was sent to the area in 1841 by the War Department to investigate this situation. The Indians of all the Five Civilized Tribes (each tribe occupied a different part of the Territory) were suffering, he found, but it was because the contractors employed by the government to feed them had instead been shamelessly cheating them. Hitchcock sent a secret report back to Washington documenting over one hundred cases of bribery, forgery, instances where rotten meat and grain had been issued, and other examples of fraud practiced against the helpless Indians. When some members of Congress later tried to obtain a copy of this report to investigate the way things were handled in Indian Territory, they were told it had "mysteriously disappeared" from War Department files. It was rumored in Washington that the report had vanished because it named several people left over from Andrew Jackson's administration as among those who were defrauding the Indians.

Of the Cherokees' Principal Chief, Hitchcock said: "After much attentive observation I am of the opinion that

John Ross is an honest man and a patriot laboring for the good of his people. In the recent trouble of his nation, including the last several years, with almost unlimited opportunities, he has not enriched himself."

But such a testimonial did not help the Chief or his people. By 1841, Stand Watie had formed his own militia and retreated to the northeastern part of the Cherokees' new lands, occasionally engaging in brief gun battles with Ross partisans. Meanwhile, Indian Territory was becoming a haven for all the white outlaws and drifters in this part of the West. Law enforcement officials could not follow them across these borders; and they had found that selling bootleg whiskey to the Indians led to quick riches. The Cherokees had no power to enforce their own laws, and the federal troops in the area under the command of General Arbuckle didn't help them. There was disorder bordering on chaos. The only event that even momentarily united all the Cherokees was common grief over the passing in 1843 of the aged Sequoyah. He had died in Mexico, where he had gone to search for a lost branch of The Real People he believed had settled there long before.

The situation became so bad that President James Polk said of the Cherokees in April 1846: "I am satisfied that there is no probability that the different parties into which it is divided can ever again live together in peace and harmony .... They should be separated and live under separate governments as distinct tribes ...." At this John Ross hurried once more to Washington to ask for help from the Nation's remaining friends in Congress. Through hard bargaining he was able to defeat Polk's proposal, and by the summer had secured an agreement acceptable to all the Nation. The government agreed to pay the money promised as part of the bargain of removal and to upgrade the quality of its provisions. Stand Watie grudgingly shook hands with Ross in the President's office.

Given a short respite from the misfortune that had followed them relentlessly for so many years, the Cherokees now began to pick up the shattered pieces of their past. Their first thought, as before, was for the children who were the future of the tribe. Even in 1841, when the Nation was facing virtual civil war, the Council had passed an act providing for a system of public education, and in less than two years had managed to build eighteen schools that were the envy of white homesteaders in neighboring Kansas Territory. The Council voted also to educate and care for the large number of orphans in the Nation. By 1851 it had commissioned and built two imposing stone buildings supported by brick columns in a clearing near Park Hill. They were the Male and Female seminaries, and they would allow Cherokee students to receive higher education without having to go off to New England like a previous generation of Indian scholars.

In 1844, *The Cherokee Advocate* had been established as the Nation's newspaper, picking up where the *Cherokee Phoenix* had left off. William P. Ross, the favorite nephew John Ross had sent to Princeton to groom for a leadership role in the Nation, was the first editor. And until the end of his life the faithful Samuel Worcester continued to be the Cherokee's Messenger, printing their newspaper and turning out a steady stream of books and translations in their language and those of the other Five Civilized Tribes.

Meanwhile, Tahlequah was growing from a small, dusty crossroads into a thriving frontier town. In 1847, the Council authorized the construction of two log buildings—at a cost of five hundred dollars for the pair—for each house of the legislature. A year later, two more buildings were commissioned as offices for the Chief and the Treasurer. Soon several shops and stores had sprung up around the town square, and as a sign of permanence, a two-storied brick Supreme Court building was built, and across from it a National jail. There were two cooks on duty whenever the National Council was in session, and any Cherokee legislator or citizen present at the deliberations could eat free of charge.

The Nation made up for the bitter days of past years when its government had been outlawed, its laws nullified, and its leaders intimidated. After the reconciliation between Ross and Stand Watie, progress was rapid. By 1859, the Cherokee Nation seemed to have regained its equilibrium. Tahlequah had become the center of the reconstructed Indian republic. Thirty-two public schools were being attended by fifteen hundred students. There were over 100,000 acres in cultivation and Cherokee farmers were averaging over 35 bushels of corn an acre in the fertile bottomlands of Indian Territory. The Nation had over 240,000 head of cattle, according to the report of a U.S. Indian agent, and were exporting 50,000 head a year, worth over $1,000,000 to eastern markets. The United States Board of Indian Commissioners pointed out years later: "In proportion to their number, the Cherokees were the wealthiest people on the globe . . . . They owned immense herds, one individual owning 20,000 head of cattle, others owning 15,000, 10,000 and so on down to 300. The man who owned less was considered a poor Indian." It seemed as though the Cherokees had entered an era of peace and prosperity.

But the Cherokees were fated to be like Sisyphus, the figure in Greek mythology whom the gods condemned to an eternity of pushing a rock up the side of a mountain only to have it fall down again when he reached the top. Just as they had begun to make their own unique mark on their

88

TOP: *The Trail of Tears* as pictured by Robert Lindneux. *Courtesy of Woolaroc Museum, Bartlesville, Oklahoma.*

BOTTOM: Contemporary Cherokee home near Tahlequah, Oklahoma.

ABOVE: Two paintings by contemporary Cherokee Indians:

TOP: *Cherokee Indian Ball Game* (stickball) by Cecil Dick.

BOTTOM: *Old Cherokee Chief's Home* by Paul Rogers.

BELOW: Cherokee Indians brought to London in 1730 by Alexander Cuming; Attakullaculla ("Little Carpenter"), far right.

XE-QUO-YAH

RIGHT: Sequoyah, who originated
the Cherokee alphabet.

BOTTOM: The Cherokee alphabet.

Cherokee Alphabet.

D_a	R_e	T_i	δ_o	C_u	i_v
$S_{ga}\ O_{ka}$	F_{ge}	Y_{gi}	A_{go}	J_{gu}	E_{gv}
$\mathscr{O}_{ha}$	P_{he}	$\mathscr{J}_{hi}$	F_{ho}	Γ_{hu}	$\mathscr{G}_{hv}$
W_{la}	C_{le}	P_{li}	G_{lo}	M_{lu}	$\mathscr{A}_{lv}$
$\mathscr{F}_{ma}$	$\mathbb{O}_{me}$	H_{mi}	5_{mo}	Y_{mu}	
$O_{na}\ t_{hna}\ G_{nah}$	Λ_{ne}	h_{ni}	Z_{no}	$\mathscr{A}_{nu}$	O_{nv}
T_{qua}	$\mathscr{O}_{que}$	$\mathscr{P}_{qui}$	V_{quo}	$\mathscr{O}_{quu}$	E_{quv}
$U_{sa}\ \mathscr{O}_s$	4_{se}	b_{si}	$\ddagger_{so}$	$\mathscr{E}_{su}$	R_{sv}
$L_{da}\ W_{ta}$	$S_{de}\ \mathbb{C}_{te}$	$\mathscr{J}_{di}\ \mathscr{J}_{ti}$	A_{do}	S_{du}	$\mathscr{O}_{dv}$
$\mathscr{S}_{dla}\ L_{tla}$	L_{tle}	C_{tli}	$\mathscr{A}_{tlo}$	$\mathscr{D}_{tlu}$	P_{tlv}
G_{tsa}	V_{tse}	I_{tsi}	K_{tso}	J_{tsu}	C_{tsv}
G_{wa}	$\mathscr{O}_{we}$	O_{wi}	$\mathscr{O}_{wo}$	$\mathscr{D}_{wu}$	6_{wv}
ω_{ya}	$\mathscr{B}_{ye}$	$\mathscr{D}_{yi}$	h_{yo}	G_{yu}	B_{yv}

Sounds represented by Vowels.

a, as a in father, or short as a in rival   *o, as aw in law, or short as o in not*
e, as a in hate, or short as e in met   *u, as oo in fool, or short as u in pull*
i, as i in pique, or short as i in pit   *v, as u in but, nasalized*

Consonant Sounds

*g nearly as in English, but approaching to k. d nearly as in English but approaching
to t. h,k,l,m,n,q,s,t,w,y, as in English. Syllables beginning with g except Ǥ have sometimes the
power of k,A,S,Ǥ are sometimes sounded to, tu, tv. and Syllables written with tl except Ǥ
sometimes vary to dl.*

Old Cherokee Capitol,
Tahlequah, Oklahoma.

BELOW: Students at Cherokee
Male Seminary, class of 1885.

Students of the Cherokee Female Seminary,
Park Hill, Oklahoma, in front of Seminary (TOP),
and in forest (BOTTOM). May 7, 1851.

TOP: First train leaving the line north of Orlando for Perry during the run for claims of September 16, 1893, showing covered wagons traveling parallel with the train.

MIDDLE: "The Run," September 16, 1893.

BOTTOM: The 1889 run for claims from Purcell, Indian Territory across the South Canadian River.

ABOVE LEFT: The Ridge
(Major Ridge)
ABOVE RIGHT: John Ridge
RIGHT: John Ross as a young man

ABOVE LEFT: Stand Watie

ABOVE RIGHT: Redbird Smith (seated) and a friend

LEFT: William Wayne Keeler

John Ross

Mrs. John Ross,
Elizabeth Brown Henley Ross,
known as "Quatie"

new land, misfortune struck again. In 1861, as the guns of Fort Sumter sounded the beginning of the bloodiest conflict in American history, the Cherokees found themselves irresistibly drawn to its center. They had seen the white man's Civil War coming and hoped to stay at its edge, waiting for it to play itself out. But the Nation was now caught up in the web of white history. Even though its strands were invisible, they were strong. And the more the Cherokees struggled for their independence, the more entangled they became.

John Ross was seventy years old when the war broke out. His brown hair had gone snowy white in the years he had served the Nation, and he now walked with a slight stoop. The people had given him an Indian name, *Coowees-coowee,* a word describing a mysterious white bird. He had recognized that the Civil War would be a catastrophe and earnestly hoped to be able to steer his government on a neutral course. Even though he and most of the people sympathized with the North, he said, "Our duty is to stand by our rights—allow no interference in our internal affairs from any source, comply with all our engagements, and rely upon the Union for justice and protection."

But the Indians were not allowed to remain aloof for long. They were pressured by the Confederacy to join its cause. The South wanted Indian Territory as a vantage point against the Union forces and because its troops were so close, had quickly coerced the other Five Civilized Tribes into making treaties with them. On the other side was the North, obliged by the 1835 Treaty of New Echota to protect the Cherokees from such intimidation, but busy fighting other battles at the onset of the war. Again the Cherokees stood alone; and soon the factionalism which had become the Nation's one weakness sprang up again.

The Civil War brought to the surface tensions among the Cherokees that had been suppressed in prior years as the Nation had gone from one crisis to another. During the fight against removal, the Cherokees—both full bloods and mixed bloods—had been able to ignore the widening differences in outlook and lifestyle that separated them. They were united in the desperate venture to save their homeland, and all else was subordinate to that great national emergency. But once they had been marched to Indian Territory, there was no longer anything that could hide the fact that these two groups had less and less in common.

Generally, mixed bloods were "progressive" and receptive to the white man's technology; full bloods continued to be traditionalists in their world view, the old men telling the children the same tales of the beginning of the world that they always had. Mixed bloods spoke English; full bloods scorned it as the enemy's language. Mixed bloods accumulated more and more wealth, bringing with them to Indian Territory the desire to enclose large tracts of land and to build plantations; full bloods wanted only a cabin and the chance to farm a few acres communally with their neighbors. Full bloods did not care that mixed bloods tended to fancy themselves a Cherokee elite; what bothered them more was the fact that by buying slaves (there were about three thousand in the Cherokee Nation when the war broke out, mainly owned by a few wealthy planters) and otherwise imitating neighboring whites, mixed bloods threatened the traditions which had always guided the people.

The war exploded these tensions in open conflict. By 1861, Stand Watie had organized a band of Confederate sympathizers who called themselves The Knights of the Golden Circle. Comprised of remnants of the Treaty Party who still hoped for revenge against John Ross, as well as wealthy mixed bloods who actively supported the Southern cause, Watie's band immediately provoked a reaction among full bloods, who quickly formed their own secret organization. They called it the Keetowah Society, choosing an old sacred name as a reminder that Cherokee traditions were menaced by such peculiar institutions as slavery. These Keetowahs did not understand the complex reasons behind the Civil War. They did not like Northern soldiers any better than those who wore gray. It did not matter why the whites were fighting, brother against brother. The war was an opportunity to purge the tribe of alien ways once and for all. Later on, when these full bloods went into battle alongside Union troops, they wore strips of corn husk tied in their hair. When two of them met, one asked, "Who are you?" and the password reply was, "I am Keetowah's son."

The war had begun badly for Northern forces. They had lost major battles, including one at nearby Wilson's Creek, Missouri. Ross appealed again and again to the federal government for protection from the Confederacy, which increased its pressure on the Cherokees to sign a treaty, but he was ignored. There were rumors that Watie's band—which had now been armed by the Southerners—would secede from the Cherokee Nation, name their leader Principal Chief, and stage a coup d'etat with the support of Confederate troops. The old Chief knew that this would mean a bloodbath in Cherokee country. "Dissension is weakness, misery, ruin," he wearily reminded his people. But he had no alternative and late in 1861 he finally gave in and reluctantly agreed to the treaty the South pressed upon the tribe. He realized the bitter irony of making common cause with some of the very people who had ruthlessly stolen Cherokee lands twenty-five years earlier. But there was no choice. Ross saw the dilemma in these terms: "We are in the position of a man standing alone upon a low spot of ground with the water rising rapidly all around him . . . . If he remains where he is, he will be swept away and perish. But then the tide carries him a drifting log. By refusing it he is a doomed man. By seizing it . . . he may be able to keep his head above water until rescued, or drift to where he can help himself."

By 1862, however, the Nation was in a state of chaos. Stand Watie had become a Confederate officer and had enlisted an Indian unit in the South's army (he eventually attained the rank of general and gained momentary fame for being the last Confederate general to surrender formally to U.S. Grant). Meanwhile Union troops, aided by volunteer contingents composed of Keetowah full bloods, made a series of uncertain forays into Cherokee country. They had been informed that despite the treaty, Ross and an overwhelming majority of the Cherokees felt no real loyalty to the South. (Indeed, at the onset of the Civil War, President Abraham Lincoln had said of Indian Territory: "There is only one man there upon whom I now rely for strength and loyalty . . . . He is John Ross, Chief of the Cherokees.")

Although Union troops didn't succeed in finally occupying Indian Territory until 1865, late in 1862 they made a sortie into the Park Hill area and took Ross into custody. Carrying the Nation's records with him, the old Chief was conducted to Kansas and from there to Washington, where he stayed until the end of the war. He struck up a friendship with President Lincoln, who saw much of his own anguish mirrored in the hard decisions the Cherokee leader had been forced to make. In their talks Ross was treated not as a traitor or a prisoner of war, but as a head of state whose authority had been temporarily usurped by the Confederacy.

Until the end of the war, the Cherokees watched helplessly as their homeland was torn apart, with Stand Watie's men occupying Tahlequah, fighting the full bloods and finally securing a chance to humiliate Ross's friends and relatives. Watie got himself elected Principal Chief and Elias Cornelius Boudinot, son of the executed leader, was appointed the Confederate Cherokee Nation's delegate to the Confederate Congress. The situation among the Cherokees went from bad to worse as chaos spread and bloodshed became an everyday occurrence. One white resident living among the Indians observed, "It seems all the time like one great funeral."

Ross tried to work for the tribe from Washington. During audiences at the White House, Lincoln reassured the aged Chief that he fully understood that the Cherokees had been coerced into an alliance with the South. "The Confederate treaty should never rise up in judgment against the Cherokees," he told Ross as the war slowly ground to an end, "nor stand in the way of perfect justice being done." But Lincoln was soon assassinated, and any chance the Indians might have had for fair treatment died with him.

In August 1865, John Ross finally returned to his people after an absence of nearly four years. On his journey back to Indian Territory, he had a panoramic view of a country cruelly devastated by war. He saw disfigured soldiers of both armies slowly making their way home and the freed slaves wandering through the countryside hungry and bewildered. He saw whole fields turned into graveyards. But he found his own Nation even more scarred by the conflict than the rest of the country. One-third of all Cherokee women were widows; one out of every four children was an orphan. Orderly government had long since vanished and lawless bands ranged the countryside pillaging what little the Indians had left. A census showed that only 13,556 Cherokees had survived the war. Again the tribe had seen its numbers drastically reduced by death and destruction. But as the old Chief watched the countryside slipping by while his coach moved toward Tahlequah, he must have thought also about his personal loss, especially the son who had died in a Confederate prisoner-of-war camp. Before he reached the ruins of his Park Hill home, Ross wrote sadly to a niece, "I find myself a stranger and homeless in my own country . . . . The picture is painful to my feelings."

Over 300,000 cattle had been stolen from the Nation and run over the border into Kansas; in some cases officers of the supposedly friendly Union Army had taken part in the theft. Testifying before the U. S. Congress, William P. Ross, editor of *The Cherokee Advocate*, noted that when the war began there were an estimated sixteen thousand hogs on Cherokee lands; but by the end, "there was not a hog nor the footprint of one to be found in the country." The prosperity the Nation had worked so hard to establish in their new home had vanished.

Ross had given up any hope that Lincoln's wishes for a just peace—at least for the Cherokees—would be honored. That promise was one of many that evaporated in the postwar cynicism. Ross sensed that the U.S. government would now force the kind of agreement on the Cherokees that was made only with a conquered people. Even though the Cherokees had tried desperately to get Union forces to protect them so they wouldn't fall victim to the Confederates, they were now to be punished by a treaty. The situation was almost unbelievable; perhaps it put the old Chief in mind of a bitter editorial that had appeared in *The Cherokee Advocate* before the war. Noting that whites were rapidly settling around the Nation, the newspaper had predicted that someday "a commissioner will be sent down to negotiate with a pocket full of money and a mouth full of lies. Some chiefs he will bribe, some he will flatter, and some he will make drunk. The result will be something that will be called a treaty."

When Ross arrived, he found that D. H. Cooley, the U.S. Commissioner in charge of the treaty negotiations, did not bother with bribes, flattery, or drink. He simply charged the Cherokees with "crimes of secession." It did not matter that an 1863 report by the federal government's Indian Bureau had already exonerated the Cherokees. It had stated ". . . for many months they steadfastly resisted efforts made by the rebels to induce them to abandon their allegiance to the Federal Government. But being wholly unprotected and without means of resistance, they were finally compelled to enter into treaty stipulations with rebel authorities. This connection was, however, of short duration, for upon the first appearance of United States forces in their country, they . . . came over to us . . . and have on several occasions proved themselves faithful and efficient soldiers." As before and since, Indian history was to be rewritten. Now that North and South had reconciled, America was united in looking west. Indian Territory, once thought to be part of what was called the Great American Desert, was now a strategic step in the westward movement; the Indians were in the way, and this was a convenient opportunity to take care of the problem they presented.

D. H. Cooley began by calling Ross a traitor and said that he must be removed from the Chieftainship he had never relinquished. (Stand Watie had been made Chief in an illegal meeting of the Council under the guns of war.) Cooley made his charge in a September 8, 1865 public meeting at the Tahlequah Council house. When he heard it, the old leader stood up ramrod straight and faced his accuser. There was silence as he fought back the tears of anger that

95

welled up in his eyes. "I have been forty odd years Chief of the Cherokees," he sternly reminded the impudent white man. "I have been elected time after time. They reelected me in my absence and I came back to the Council at my advanced age, after burying my wife and burying my son. I had three sons in your army, also three grandsons and three nephews. . . . I have borne a reputation that I have maintained up to the present time, sir, which is dearer to me than my life."

Cooley ignored Ross. He went on to describe the proposed treaty. It sounded as if it had been made by a surveyor: the Nation would be divided into southern and northern branches, each with its own separate government; there would be a cession of Cherokee lands (near the Kansas border) to the federal government; the railroads now hovering on the outskirts of Indian Territory would be allowed to enter its borders; and the Cherokees would have to relinquish their independence and join with the other tribes of the area in a single territorial government ruled over by a white man.

The Cherokees had murmured angrily when Cooley insulted their chief. They were awestruck when he finished reading these provisions and then appointed Elias Cornelius Boudinot, former Confederate sympathizer, as the Cherokee who would be in charge of treaty negotiations. The Indians were shocked because they knew that the younger Boudinot had not only been a traitor in the past, but now favored the treaty only because he had been hired as a lobbyist by the railroads.

Once again John Ross made the long, hard journey east to argue for his people. After pleading their case before Congress and the President, he had one last victory, although a small one. As a result of his efforts, some of the harsher features of the 1866 treaty were eliminated, including the provisions to split the Nation and put it under a single territorial government. But even the clever diplomacy of the old Chief couldn't keep the railroads out, or prevent some of the Cherokee lands from being taken.

As always, John Ross had done his best. Harsh though it was, the treaty he negotiated brought the Nation he had served so long another forty years of life. In the past Ross had seen his people triumph. But he had also seen them suffer and die, and he wondered if all the toil and heartache had been worth it. Weren't the Cherokees closer to being a conquered people than when they had worn the breechcloth and blanket back in the old country? Wasn't the future more uncertain than ever? John Ross knew that his people were about to step over a dangerous and crucial threshold once again. But this time he wouldn't be going with them. Less than two weeks after negotiating the treaty, the man who had defied Presidents while serving his people for fifty of his seventy-six years laid his burden down, dying in his sleep in Washington on August 1, 1866.

When they could, the people had Ross's body moved to the small cemetery where it rests today. The eulogy read at his funeral showed their appreciation for the long and faithful years he had given them. "He never sacrificed the interests of his nation to expediency," it said. "He never lost sight of the welfare of the people. For them he labored daily for a long life; and upon them he bestowed his last expressed thoughts . . . . His words are inseparable from the history of the Cherokee people for nearly half a century. His example in the daily walks of life will linger on in the future and whisper words of hope."

In the years to come, such words would be badly needed.

V.
The Limits
of the Earth

The famous French traveler and writer Alexis de Tocqueville had been journeying through America in the 1830s when the Cherokees were fighting removal. Like others, he watched with disbelief as events unfolded. But this keen observer of the men and institutions of the New World was even more disturbed by what he heard than by what he saw. To his surprise, many of the Americans he spoke to refused to admit that what was taking place was indeed a tragedy—not only for the Cherokees, but also for the whole country. Instead they accepted the excuse Jackson and his politicians offered: Indian removal was actually a blessing in disguise; it would give the Cherokees and the other Five Civilized Tribes room to go their own way in a faraway land where the white man wouldn't bother them. After all, hadn't Jackson's Secretary of War John Eaton assured the Indians as they were being driven out of Georgia: "If you will go to the setting sun you will be happy; there you can remain in peace and quietness; as long as the oaks grow that country shall be guaranteed to you and no white man shall be permitted to settle near you."

But de Tocqueville was doubtful. There had been many promises made to the Cherokees in the past and every one of them had been broken. He saw even greater misery in their future. "Who can assure them that they will at length be allowed to dwell in peace in their new retreat?" he asked. "The United States pledge themselves to maintain them there; but in a few years the same white population which now flocks around them will doubtless track them anew . . . . They will then be exposed to the same evils . . . and as the limits of the earth will at last fail them, their only refuge is the grave."

In the years following the death of John Ross, when their new lands were again invaded by whites and it seemed that they would once again be dispossessed, the Cherokees also wondered if there was any haven where they would be safe from the grasping American. They heard rumors of the war of extermination being waged by George Armstrong Custer and other military commanders in the plains states, and were glad that their tribe was no longer considered "savage." Yet they faced an attack less sudden but almost as devastating. In the short space of forty years, from 1866 to 1906, the Cherokees saw the destruction of the nation they had labored so hard to build and the very real possibility of their social death as a people.

Times were changing. After the Civil War the Cherokee Nation was no longer a significant power inside America. There were no more great men like John Ross to do battle with the might of the U.S. government, no more epic clashes over questions like removal. The Cherokees strug-

gled as much as they could against events which now over-
whelmed them, but no one besides themselves seemed to
care any more. They probably appreciated the statement
made by Chief Joseph of the Nez Percés, captured in 1879
after a long and daring defiance of the U.S. Army. Weary
and depressed by the loss of many of his people, he threw
down his rifle and said sadly, "I will fight no more forever."
It was not the will Indians lacked, but a way.

After the Civil War, the country was exhausted, not only
because it had just finished the bloodiest fighting in its history, but also because of the moral fever the question of
slavery had aroused. The dream of reshaping the racist and
autocratic society of the South by a thoroughgoing Recon-
struction evaporated; by the 1870s the idealism of the aboli-
tionists had given way to the cynicism of the administration
of President Ulysses S. Grant. It was the Gilded Age. A new
breed of businessmen began to direct the country's destiny;
graft and corruption were the order of the day.

With one national scandal after another assaulting the
country's sensibilities, the discovery that an "Indian Ring"
had taken over the government's administration of Indian
Affairs in the 1860s was hardly surprising. This secret group
of contractors, Indian agents, and local politicians made huge
profits from filling contracts to provide beef and other provisions to the tribes, handing out annuities (the yearly payment of goods stipulated in treaties), and taking care of other
aspects of the government's responsibilities to the Cherokees
and other Indians. By 1873, an estimated $500,000 of gov-
ernment money earmarked for Indians had been paid out
in fraudulent and irregular claims to whites. Corruption
stretched from the lowest-paid Indian agent working in the
field to the highest appointed officials. It was discovered that

the man who became Grant's Commissioner of Indian Affairs had earlier bilked the Chippewa tribe out of large sums when he was their agent by selling their timber at low prices to friends who gave him a kickback on their profits. Such opportunities for profiteering explained why the seemingly unappealing job of being an Indian agent for some tribe on the lonely frontier was considered a political prize: it allowed a variety of more lucrative rewards.

But the United States built up a tolerance for such practices as it returned to the national task from which the Civil War had temporarily diverted it: the settlement of the West and expansion of its influence into the Pacific. In 1862 the Homestead Act had been passed, allowing up to 160 free acres of government land to every settler; and in the next twenty years, over 50,000,000 acres went from the "public domain" to private ownership. There were also lavish grants of land to the railroad corporations which were to connect the East and the West.

The role of the U.S. Cavalry was to clear Indians out of the way so that there would be a public domain to give out. The Cherokees watched the plains states, where horse soldiers waged total warfare that often didn't distinguish women and children from warriors. Over the next decade the Indian Wars proved a costly business. An 1870 Congressional investigation revealed that over $1 million was spent for each Indian killed, but the American people accepted this figure as a necessary expense in attaining their manifest destiny.

The last desperate efforts of Sitting Bull, Crazy Horse, and the other Sioux leaders, Chief Joseph of the Nez Percé, and the Apache Geronimo were yet to come. General George Armstrong Custer had not yet met his fate on a wind-swept knoll in the hills of Montana. But already Indians were being treated like a conquered people. Since it was not necessary to make treaties with the vanquished (even treaties that could be broken whenever it became expedient), the U.S. Senate decided in 1871 that in the future Indian affairs would be handled by legislation only. There would be no more treaty negotiations, which meant in effect that laws regulating Indians would be pushed through by Congressmen from the western states without much objection from their eastern colleagues, who wanted similar regional privileges on issues of concern to themselves. Nothing the Indians could do or say made any difference. As the great Sioux chief Red Cloud remarked at about this time, "I have sent a great many words to the Great Father, but they never reached him. They were drowned on the way."

Even the Five Civilized Tribes, which had more power and prestige than other Indians, suffered. America no longer needed to deal with Indian tribes as nations having certain rights. Now they were only an obstruction blocking the white man's superior destiny. The temper of the times is seen in an 1867 editorial in a Kansas newspaper. It read: "Indians are a set of miserable, dirty, lousy, blanketed, thieving, lying, sneaking, murdering, graceless, faithless, gut-eating skunks ... whose immediate and final extermination all men, except for Indian agents and traders, should pray for."

During this ominous era the Cherokees tried to reconstruct their war-ravaged Nation. William P. Ross, who had inherited the mantle of leadership from his uncle, admonished the people to carry on. "Let us look forward upon the pleasing landscape of the future," he said, "and not upon the dark valley of the past, with its lost friends, blighted hopes, and sad and fearful associations." They had been hurt badly by the Civil War and the Treaty of 1866, he admitted, and the ring was tightening around them; but they still had their national sovereignty and their will as a people, so the Cherokees looked ahead. Once again they turned their attention to the schools that had been the finest west of the Mississippi. During the Civil War, some Cherokees in refugee camps had set up temporary schools; otherwise the children would have missed five years in their education. But by 1867 the Nation had reopened thirty-two public schools, and three years later there were sixty-four. The Council came up with other far-reaching programs, commissioning the construction of a national orphanage to take care of the children who had lost parents in the disastrous events of recent years, and making plans to build a national asylum for the insane.

But while the people could rebuild their old institutions and plan new ones, they could not ignore the signs all around them. The Cherokees bravely carried on as if their tomorrows were numberless, but they knew that they weren't. Their country was on the verge of being opened up and they were powerless to do anything about it. As the Pacific Coast was settled, the last generation of frontiersmen began to cast hungry looks toward Indian Territory and its huge expanses of virgin land.

The 1866 Treaty had forced the Nation to grant rights of way to the railroads. And in June 1870, the Missouri, Kansas and Texas line had reached the northern border of Indian Territory. Two years later the Atlantic and Pacific Railroad had cut a westward path across Cherokee country. Shortly afterward it began to agitate for legislation—as the corporation's directors said—"so that the rich and desirable lands of Indian Territory, now laying waste, may be occupied and utilized by the white population and thereby promote the construction of railroads . . . ." Stockholders of the Missouri, Kansas and Texas railroad (including John D. Rockefeller and J. P. Morgan, the "robber barons" of a later era) were quick to realize that if the U.S. government were to take ownership of the Territory out of Indian hands, then the railroad could do as it pleased with the valuable twenty-mile-wide strip of land it had been granted—subject to continuing Indian title—to construct its line. As long as the tribes continued to own the Territory, this land could not be sold or developed except for the laying of railroad track. Hadn't the Union Pacific already been given twelve million acres in the Plains states, they pointed out, and the Central Pacific nine million? Weren't other railroads being allowed to build up the huge pieces of public domain they had obtained in the rest of the country?

Every session of Congress saw more bills introduced to change the status of Indian Territory. None of them had yet been passed, but the railroads stepped up their pressure. Their lobbying activities became so excessive that in 1872 a committee of the U.S. House of Representatives observed: "[It] springs from the fact that Congress, in an unwise moment, granted many millions of acres belonging to the Indians to railroad corporations . . . . And now these soulless corporations hover like greedy cormorants over this territory, inviting Congress to remove all restraint and allow them to sweep down and swallow over 23 million acres of land . . . . Why must we do this? In order that corporations may be enriched and the railroad stocks advanced on Wall Street."

In the more than three decades they had been in Indian Territory, the Cherokees had sent deep roots down into their new land. It was rich in timber, game, and other resources. There were great pine forests on the mountain slopes, and stands of strong blackjack oak in the valleys. The herds of buffalo and elk that had been there when the first Old Settlers arrived at the turn of the century had long since been hunted out, but there was a profusion of other animals, and a U.S. surveying team called it "one of the prime game refuges in the country." The soil and the climate were good. The land seemed as though it could support the Indians' way of life forever. As one full blood told some white visitors, "We raise our corn and wheat; we have hogs, cattle, and plenty of chickens. We may be poor, but we can go anywhere and find enough to eat . . . . The people don't care to go elsewhere."

But day by day the face of their country was changing. Soon it would take on the same worn look as other places the white man had walked. When the railroad lines criss-crossed Indian lands, priceless timber suddenly vanished, the work gangs cutting it down haphazardly to use in their construction and to sell for extra money. In 1879 a Cherokee delegation complained to Congress that "parties came in and cut and removed immense quantities of walnut timber . . . . On one single occasion, we observed a train of cars loaded with it." The wild turkey, bear, deer, and other animals the Indians relied on for food became scarce when white hunters and sportsmen began arriving on the rail lines that had penetrated to the heart of the Nation.

But the most drastic change of all was the invasion after the Civil War by hordes of whites who obviously meant to stay permanently on the lands of the Five Civilized Tribes. Following Emancipation, some of the wealthy mixed bloods had been forced to hire white laborers to replace the slaves who had worked their large farms. Now the towns that sprang up overnight at each railroad terminus were quickly populated by shopkeepers and workers. Whites set up businesses, married Cherokees so they could legally acquire lands, or just claimed squatters' rights to obtain a piece of the Nation's property, knowing that it was only a matter of time until the government took jurisdiction over the area. The

Cherokees called these people "intruders." By 1880 there were six thousand of them, and less than ten years later they far outnumbered the Indians. In 1893, the first federal census of Indian Territory showed over 100,000 whites and barely 50,000 Indians.

Fearing it would drown in a sea of whites, the Nation set up a citizenship court to determine which of the foreigners had a right to reside among them. It asked for help from federal officials to expel those who didn't, but such requests were ignored. Even if the government had wanted to help it would have had to declare a state of martial law to do anything about the problem. The intruders had come to stay. They built farms and turned their cattle loose on the Cherokees' open range. As an added insult they even published newspapers agitating for the federal government to take control over the Territory and thus legitimate their claims.

This situation was further vexed by the existence of several million "unassigned" acres in the western half of Indian Territory. These had been the westernmost lands of the Creek and Seminole nations when the Five Civilized Tribes first arrived there. But in the 1866 negotiations following the Civil War, they had become the spoils of war when the federal government took them as part of the price for Indian "collaboration" with the Confederacy. At that time the architects of federal Indian policy had thought to use this area to receive tribes to be moved down from the rapidly growing plains states. In other words, it was to be a dumping ground for Indians in the path of the westward movement. In 1867, the Sac and Fox Indians had been moved from Kansas to the northeastern corner of this area; not long afterward, bands of the Cheyenne and Arapaho tribes had been forced out of their mountain homes and taken to its northwestern corner. The Comanches and

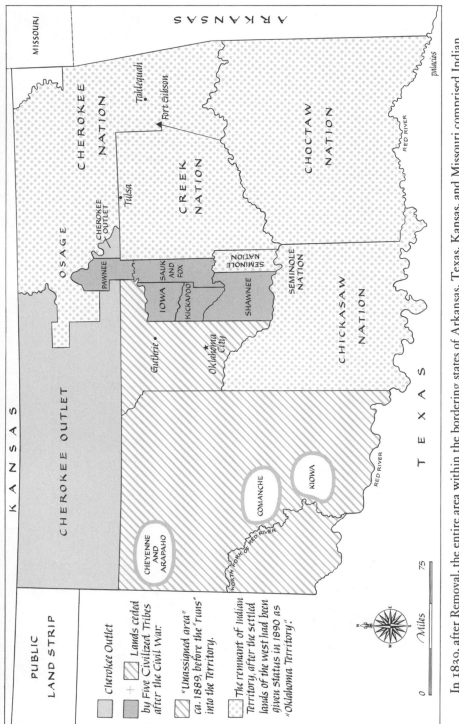

In 1839, after Removal, the entire area within the bordering states of Arkansas, Texas, Kansas, and Missouri comprised Indian Territory. At the end of the Civil War, the western half of the Territory was taken from the Five Civilized Tribes by the U.S. government. Some of it was assigned to tribes that were endemic to the area or to those relocated from the Plains states; the remainder was opened to white settlement in 1888. This map shows how Indian Territory was divided at that time.

other people indigenous to Indian Territory were also assigned permanent homes here.

The government planned to settle other tribes in the "unassigned" area. But the Indian Wars of the 1870s showed that it was easier and cheaper simply to shunt defeated Indian nations to barren reservations in their own locale than to move them hundreds of miles to Indian Territory. This decision left five million acres where no tribes had been relocated. In the future, the term "unassigned" or "public" lands referred only to this part of Indian Territory. By 1880, settlers in covered wagons were converging from all directions on this land, which had already been christened "Oklahoma." They had read handbills advertising free land which had been printed up and distributed by the railroads. The Indians' fate was becoming clear.

David Payne, a broad-shouldered farmer's son with a mustache drooping down over the sides of his mouth, was in his middle age when he became the unofficial leader of the "Boomers," the name given to settlers who hungered for what they began calling "public lands" lying vacant in Indian Territory. Payne had been a soldier, jailbird, part-time politician, and Kansas rancher, and by 1879 the footloose westerner had formed an organization he called The Oklahoma Colony, which promised to lead the faithful into a New Jerusalem in the wilderness. He charged dues of two dollars a year; another two dollars surveying fee allowed any member of the colony a 160-acre claim when the area was finally opened up. Business was brisk. By 1881 Payne enrolled fourteen thousand members. They wanted action, and their leader tried to give it to them. Time and again he led his Boomers in small groups over the boundary of Indian Territory into the "unassigned" lands. Overnight they founded tent towns with names like New Philadelphia which lasted a few days, until the U.S. Cavalry escorted them out of the area in accordance with President Rutherford B. Hayes's 1880 proclamation that no part of Indian Territory was open to settlement.

But Payne and his followers were undaunted. After all, it had also once been said that the Black Hills of South Dakota would never be opened to settlers. But in 1874 Custer had accompanied prospectors there along what the Sioux came to call "The Thieves' Trail," and when tens of thousands of whites with gold fever had followed, the government had sent in the army, not to expel them but to protect them from the Indians. The Boomers knew that time was on their side. And in their own way, they were as convinced of the righteousness of their cause as the Puritans had been when they settled Indian land two hundred and fifty years earlier. A member of The Oklahoma Colony, an ordained minister, once preached a Sunday sermon to Payne's assembled multitude comparing President Hayes to Pharaoh, Oklahoma to the Promised Land, and the Boomers to the Lord's own people.

Pressured on one side by the railroads and on the other by people like David Payne, the federal government finally gave in and agreed to open to the public nearly three thousand square miles of these "unassigned" lands. In April 22, 1889, thousands of people massed on the borders ready to claim their share of this bounty. It was only the first of several dramatic runs for land in Oklahoma that would be held over the next few years. The eager mass was restrained from leaving before the signal by squadrons of cavalry, but some (the "Sooners," who would one day become Oklahoma's symbol) still managed to leave "sooner" than the rest. As a volley of gunfire rang out at high noon all along the starting line, those assembled began the mad rush for free land. A year later there were sixty thousand people residing there. Those settlers who came too late for this run spilled over as squatters on the lands that had been set aside for the Cheyennes and other transplanted tribes. Recognizing that the western half of what had once been Indian Territory was now occupied and controlled by whites, Congress gave this area official status as Oklahoma Territory. For a decade it would coexist with the remainder of Indian Territory, which still belonged to the Five Civilized Tribes; then the two would be forcibly merged into the state of Oklahoma.

At first the Cherokees were passive witnesses to the spectacle of whites invading Indian land. The fact that it was not their land that the Boomers settled in 1889 was only small comfort, for they knew that they were witnessing just the first act of a longer drama. Soon it would be their turn. The Nation owned over six million acres that were not occupied. This area, below the Kansas border, was called the "Cherokee Outlet," and for years the Council had been leasing it to a group of Texas cattlemen who paid $100,000 a year to graze their stock there. The money was put to good use to run the government and schools. But every day more settlers were coming west to clamor for free land, and the government told the Cherokees that they must sell the Outlet. The Council refused. But after being harassed by federal commissioners who spent six months at Tahlequah and flatly forbade their leasing the lands any longer, the Cherokees finally capitulated early in 1893 and sold the outlet to the government. The Cherokees were paid $1.25 an acre for their holdings.

On September 16, 1893, the Outlet was opened to the public in what eyewitnesses said was the most spectacular of all the "runs" into Indian Territory. An on-the-spot observer looking through field glasses at the people held back at the starting point remembered seeing a human line that stretched to the horizon. Individual riders and families waited in covered wagons one hundred yards deep; the horses were taut and ready to race for the twenty thousand claims into which the area had been divided. A correspondent for a small local newspaper, *The Fort Smith Elevator,* described what happened when the run began: "At 12 o'clock a volley of gunfire ran along the northern and southern lines of the land which for nearly half a century had been coveted by the pale face . . . . Even before the firing had ceased, the columns had moved. There were race horses trained to speed . . . that were ridden by men either in the employ of townsite or cattle companies . . . . The homesteaders relied on their best stock, but were distanced at the start.

"The Atchison, Topeka and Santa Fe train left the border line at exactly the stroke of 12, loaded down and running over with struggling, perspiring humanity. People could not be kept off the train. There were not enough troops quartered there, if all of them had been concentrated at this point, to have kept out the men determined to go.

"The opening was signalized with a large number of tragedies. Several men were shot in quarrels over claims. Four men were killed by soldiers for starting on the strip before the hour of noon arrived. Several were thrown from their horses and either crushed or trampled to death. Among the latter victims were 3 or 4 women."

The Five Civilized Tribes looked on with a shudder. If the whites could run over and crush each other to get land, what would they do to Indians standing in the way?

An era was coming to a close, and the Cherokees sensed that a point of no return had been passed. The Nation had been menaced before and had always managed to survive.

But this time was different, and the Cherokees, especially the full-blood traditionalists, felt that more than Indian land was threatened. The old way of life was in danger now. It was about this time that the anthropologist James Mooney visited the tribe. He talked to the old men and women who thought they might be the last to know and live by the wisdom of The Real People. One of those he spoke to was the aged *A'Yun'ini*, called Swimmer, who had been trained by the *Adawehi* when he was young. Wearing an old-style turban and carrying the terrapin shell rattle that was his badge of priestly authority at communal ceremonies, the frail and dignified full-blood patriarch reminisced with Mooney about the past. He told how the holy relics of the tribe—the great peace pipe carved of white stone with seven stems, one for each of the clans, the sacred drum cut in the shape of a turtle that had once hung in the townhouse of Keeowe, the box covered in deerskin that had held the tribe's most precious things—had disappeared one by one. It was as if the people had fallen out of the good graces of the Great Spirit. "All the old things are gone now," Swimmer said sadly, "and the Indians are different."

The Indians had indeed changed. The factionalism that followed the making of the New Echota treaty was long since dead. It had disappeared in the aftermath of the Civil War with the passing of John Ross and the retreat of Stand Watie to a remote corner of the Nation where he finished his life in peaceful obscurity as a gentleman farmer. But if the old rivalry was gone, that other, even more fundamental division between mixed bloods and full bloods had become so complete that there was no longer any way to bridge it.

By the 1880s mixed bloods, who were increasingly hard to distinguish from their white neighbors, had taken control of the Cherokee Nation's government. Ever since the turn of the century when the tribe had decided to make its great experiment with the white man's ways, mixed bloods had been valuable spokesmen in expressing the full bloods' hopes and needs to the white man and in arguing for those views in courts and Congress. However, it had been the genius of John Ross to understand that the mixed blood stood between two worlds and, unlike the full blood, had no unique vision that was worthy of protection. But after this great leader's death, the mixed bloods, because of their education and polish, gradually took over the offices and direction of the Nation. They still claimed to be interested in protecting the lands and heritage of the full blood; they never turned their backs on him. But finally, it was their own view of things, not his, that the Nation's government expressed.

The full bloods had accepted much of the white man's world, but still lived according to older patterns in small settlements along mountain stream beds. The influence of the clans, which once controlled Cherokee social life, had almost disappeared, but each settlement had a ceremonial center—usually the local Cherokee Baptist Church—where the rituals and traditions that had always held the people together were still practiced.

The Cherokee full blood had not been happy to see the Nation's government slip out of his control, but there was no move to sell the people's lands, and William P. Ross and others in the long line of mixed-blood chiefs who followed John Ross had never flagrantly abused their powers. Moreover, the full blood had never valued control of the Nation's government as an end in itself. He always regarded his government as a tool adapted from the white man to be used in the struggle to protect the old ways. As long as the interests of the people were not betrayed, it did not matter that the mixed bloods held the reins of government. But soon a series of events occurred in the white man's rush to obtain the lands of Indian Territory that once again made these questions vitally important.

In 1887, the U.S. Senate had passed the Dawes Act, a crucial piece of legislation which would determine the course of Indian history for the next fifty years. At the time it was seen as a "humanitarian" way of dealing with the "Indian problem," which everyone agreed had been worsened by subduing the tribes and sending them to desolate reservations. The architect of the new strategy, Senator Henry Dawes of Massachusetts, had decided that he knew why the Indians were sinking deeper into poverty and despair. It was not because they had been subjected to warfare and less direct kinds of violence, but because they held their lands in common. If the red man owned his lands individually, Dawes had reasoned, then he would develop the initiative to better himself. He would have his own plot of ground and work it as white homesteaders had done all over the West; like his white counterpart, he would want to own more. Ownership and happiness were indivisible. Once the Indian became successful as an individual farmer or rancher, he would become a successful American. With the appropriate action by Congress, Dawes was certain the "Indian problem" would solve itself.

Henry Dawes had a religious awe for private ownership. It was a confidence no amount of contrary evidence could shake. After visiting the Cherokees on a fact-finding tour he had admitted: "There is not a family in that whole nation that has not a home of its own, there was not a pauper in the nation, and the nation did not owe a dollar. It built its own capital . . . and it built its schools and hospitals." Yet, he added, "the defect of the system was apparent. They have got as far as they can go because they own their land in common .... There is no enterprise to make your home any better than that of your neighbor. There is no selfishness, which is at the bottom of civilization. Till the people consent to give up their lands, and divide them among their citizens so that each can own the land he cultivates, they will not make much more progress."

Seldom had the gulf separating the philosophy of the white man from that of the Indian been so explicitly expressed. Yet the Senator's vision of what was good for the red man had become law. The Dawes Act provided for the breaking up of tribal or reservation lands into allotments of 160 acres for heads of families, 80 acres for single adults, and 40 acres for children. After the Indian was given this land, if there was anything left over of the reservation—as there usually was—it was to be opened to white settlement. The tribes, of course, had opposed the plan because it was fundamentally at odds with their view of life and the environment. "The Earth is our Mother"—so went a familiar Indian saying—"and we cannot sell our mother." In the same way that it could not be sold, the earth could not be "owned." The Indians had been against the Dawes Act for more practical reasons as well: they knew that small plots owned by individuals could be taken far more easily than the large holdings of a tribe. (Time would prove them right. Despite its "humanitarian" objectives, the Dawes Act was the greatest legislative disaster ever visited on the American Indian. From its inception in 1887 until 1934, when the policy of allotment finally ceased, lands under Indian control shrank by two-thirds, from nearly 140 million acres to less than 55 million.)

But what the tribes wanted was not important to Henry Dawes. Like all passionate benefactors, he was sure he knew what was good for the objects of his charity. For once,

Westerners approved of what government was doing. When the Dawes Act sailed through Congress, it involved a marriage of the strong-armed philanthropy of the liberal Easterners and the settlers' land hunger.

Because of their prestige, the Five Civilized Tribes were able to gain exemption from the provisions of the Dawes Act for a few years. But the feeling in Congress at the beginning of the 1890s was that an Indian Territory standing alongside the more populous and progressive Oklahoma Territory was now an anachronism. Why should such a large area be held in special status for five Indian Nations? By 1893, the chaos created in Indian Territory by the railroads, the white "intruders," and the various openings of "public" lands was such that President Grover Cleveland decided it was time to solve the problem once and for all. He appointed a special commission headed by Senator Henry Dawes, now the country's "expert" in Indian Affairs, to hold meetings with the Five Civilized Tribes "for the purpose of the extinguishment of national or tribal title to lands . . . with a view . . . to the creation of a state of the Union which shall embrace the lands within Indian Territory."

For five years, the Dawes Commission talked to a stone wall of Cherokee resistance. Again, a steady stream of Cherokee representatives traveled to Washington, trying to outflank a policy they knew would have disastrous consequences for their people. But the government was determined. If the Dawes Commission could not solve the problem by negotiation, there would be legislation; and in 1898 Congress passed the Curtis Act—"for the protection of the people of Indian Territory and other purposes." The "other purposes," of course, were its real motivation, and this act dealt a death blow to the Cherokee Nation. It abolished tribal courts and laws, made the actions of the Council subject to the approval of the federal government, and forced allotment on the Indians. When news of the Curtis Act came to the Nation, T. M. Buffington, Principal Chief at the time, said sadly: "The little government we love so well and to which we have clung so tenaciously is fast going."

The mixed-blood leaders of the Nation fought the impending changes as well as they could; they opposed the Curtis Act with every legal means at their disposal and with all the moral pressure they could bring to bear. When the mixed bloods finally saw that the Nation could not win, they were not profoundly shaken: most were comfortable with the white man's ways and would fit into the new scheme of things quite well. If they had a sense of loss regarding the Cherokee Nation, and most did, it was primarily nostalgia for the past that had produced them. The difference between them and the full bloods was that the latter could not conceive of losing this crucial struggle. They felt that what was at stake was more than the loss of the Cherokee government. To them, forcing individual ownership of land was an assault on the core of the values by which they had always lived—that communal lifestyle which was the social cement that held the people together and made them as one.

The full bloods feared that this marked the destruction of their way of life, the literal end of *Ani-Yun'Wiya*, The Real People. They met and talked, at first informally in their settlements and then in larger groups throughout the Nation. The Keetowah Society, which had been born in the stress of the Civil War, was revived. The full bloods desperately cast about for a way to stop what was happening. Their movement gained a leader in a short, slender man named Redbird Smith. He had been born in 1850 and raised as a staunch traditionalist, having received instruction in the

Cherokee religion as a young man. Those Keetowahs who followed him soon came to be called "Nighthawks" because of their vigilance.

Redbird Smith talked with the Cherokees' neighbors about ways of stopping the process that seemed to be leading them all to extinction. While in the Creek Nation, he helped form the Four Mothers Society, a larger resistance organization of full bloods from all the Five Civilized Tribes. Dead set against allotment, the society used the one-dollar-a-month dues full-blood families scraped together to hire lawyers and send its own delegations to Washington. To emphasize their unity, the full bloods of all tribes joined in nightlong dances and purification rites.

When the U.S. Commissioners came to take the 1900 census and place their names on the official roll of the tribe as a first step in the division of property, the full bloods hid from them. They ran away. It was not out of fear of being hurt, but from terror at the implications of allotment. No white man and not even the mixed blood could understand the shock the full blood felt at the idea of having the land his tribe had paid for with the Trail of Tears divided up into tiny pieces. He grieved as a man without a country. It didn't matter to him that he would now "own" a certain piece of acreage, perhaps more than he had farmed before. (There had never been ownership *per se* in the Nation; a man was entitled to fence off all the land he could farm, but it belonged to the people.) For him the tragedy was that the mountains, rivers, and valleys which had belonged to all, which were the soul of the people, were now disappearing, and he was about to be forced to live inside the same kind of constricted circle as the white man. When the enrollment parties came, he tried to evade them; if this failed, he shoved his allotment certificate back into the white official's hands as if it were poison.

In 1902, Redbird Smith was arrested and imprisoned for his role in the resistance. As he remembered, "I was at home enjoying myself in peace when I and several other Indians were arrested . . . and taken to jail for standing up for our rights. On Saturday evening they put me in jail and on Sunday morning they let me out, and then they took me to the commissioner's office and made me enroll against my will." When he later went to Washington to testify before Congress, he carried the symbolic eagle feather left by his great-grandfather; he also brought with him a photographic enlargement of the original deed of Indian Territory lands to the Cherokee Nation. When he spoke, some Senators smiled indulgently and made jokes about the Indians' simple speech and naive ideas. But he represented the full-blood view of things, which saw a man—or a country—as no better than his ability to keep his word. "I say that I never will change," Smith told the legislators. "Before our God I won't. It extends to heaven, this great treaty made with the United States . . . . I can't stand and live and breathe if I take this allotment . . . . To take and put Indians on the land individually will be just the same as burying them, for they cannot live."

But it soon became clear that appeals to past promises would be no more effective than anything else in changing the white man's mind. Redbird Smith returned to his people convinced that it would be pointless to continue the fight against allotment, which the mixed-blood leaders of the Nation were finally forced to accept in 1905. They were the last of the Five Civilized Tribes to do so. Four years later, a final roll of the Nation was prepared. Many people with only a small fraction of Cherokee blood journeyed several hundred miles to Tahlequah to get their names listed. The number of Cherokees had swollen overnight. Of 41,798 on the roll, however, only 8,698 were full bloods.

But such greed didn't matter to Redbird Smith and the Keetowah leaders. They had decided that the only way to ensure the survival of the Cherokees' tribal identity was simply to withdraw to their settlements in the "Cherokee hills." It was a way of fighting back, the only way they had. They paid even more intense attention than before to their rituals and religion, and soon ceremonial centers had sprung up wherever there was a full-blood settlement. The Keetowahs knew that time was short. Soon their land would be cut up into small slices and the government that had served them for decades abolished. The mixed bloods would gradually blend in with the white man and they would be the only Cherokees left.

The final act of this drama of dispossession unfolded with almost bewildering speed and finality. In 1906 Congress passed a law for "the final disposition of the affairs of the tribes of Indian Territory." The federal government took over control of the school system which had once been the Cherokees' pride; it took power to receive and spend the Indians' money; it abolished the government the Cherokees had labored to build and keep together over the years.

There would be one thing more—statehood for the area—and that was but a short step away. The leaders of the Five Civilized Tribes knew they had no chance of stopping it, but they did hope to get Indian Territory admitted as a separate state. They held a convention, chose Sequoyah as the name for their state, and called a referendum throughout the Territory. Better than 80 percent of the fifty-six thousand people who voted favored the idea. But this was denied them as had been an earlier suggestion to allow full bloods to pick their allotments in adjacent sections and continue to hold the land in common.

At 10:16 on the morning of November 16, 1907, the long journey of the Cherokee Nation came to an end as President Theodore Roosevelt's proclamation uniting Oklahoma Territory and Indian Territory sang across the telegraph wires. The Indians' tradition of self-government was dispensed with; they were now nothing more than a vastly outnumbered minority in a state they hadn't created and didn't want. Already predatory interests were descending on them, trying to get the lands which they had been given. But there were no problems at Guthrie, the capital of the new state of Oklahoma. It was the scene of wild, often drunken celebrations during week-long ceremonies marking the event. A central moment in the festivities came when an Indian woman clothed in traditional buckskin and representing Indian Territory was given in symbolic marriage to a white man in cowboy dress representing Oklahoma Territory. When the ceremony was completed, there was dancing in the streets as guns were shot into the air.

VI.
Cherokee Autumn

In the summertime, many of the tourists traveling through Oklahoma make a point of stopping at Tahlequah. Remembering that it once was the capital of a famous Indian tribe, they get out of their cars and wander down the city's main street. In the town square they inspect the statue of Stand Watie in his general's uniform and pause to look at the gray Supreme Court building or at the National Prison, now the town jail. But there are few relics of the vanished nation that subdued the wilderness of Indian Territory 150 years ago. By and large Tahlequah is an example of the rural Americana that replaced this Indian culture and now itself seems quaintly antique. By early morning old men in bib overalls and straw hats have congregated on their benches in the park and talk in slow drawls as they shift the cuds of tobacco in their mouths from side to side. Merchants still come out at noon to lean diagonally in their doorways and gossip with their customers; and the humid summer evenings are alive with the shouts of children chasing fireflies.

Often a tourist stops one of these local residents and asks, "Whatever happened to the Cherokee tribe, anyway?" The answer is usually something vague. "Oh, we're all a little bit Indian down here," or "The Cherokees? Well, they got together with the whites and built this state." He might tell of certain famous Oklahomans with a fraction of Cherokee blood, like the entertainer Will Rogers or the oil man W. W. Keeler. Or he might advise the tourist to visit the Cherokee Cultural Center if he wants to learn more about the Indians.

So those who are especially curious get back in their cars and drive a few miles outside of town to a peaceful glade where stubs of pillars that once supported the Cherokee Female Seminary still stand. One part of this Cultural Center is a re-creation of an eighteenth-century Cherokee village. For a small fee the visitor can listen to a guide tell how the Indians lived back in Georgia and Tennessee before the white man came, and watch women in Indian dress, sitting cross-legged near mud-covered huts, stitching together skins with bone needles, husking grain in rock craters, and cooking pulpy dough over an open fire. Men wearing buckskin and wigs with long blue-black braids wander through the village working at tasks that are also centuries old—shaping logs with a stone ax into dugout canoes, or putting wild goose feathers onto the shafts of hand-made arrows.

The "inhabitants" of the village are local Indians paid by the hour for their impersonation; they are not allowed to speak English in front of the white tourists, for to do so would destroy the authenticity of the scene.

Across the way from the village is a large amphitheater

where an outdoor drama called "The Trail of Tears" is performed in the summer months by a company of white actors. This chronicle of the Cherokee past begins in Georgia, dramatizes the events leading to the tribe's expulsion and its trek to Indian Territory, and summarizes its early days here. The play ends in November 1907, when the Territory became part of the state and the Indians became Oklahomans. In the final scene, the cast joins hands to sing in praise of the good future to be enjoyed both by the red man and the white.

Like the white culture of Tahlequah, the Cherokee Cultural Center also suggests that Indians are part of a bygone era, a past that ended when their Nation was abolished and its lands cut up into thousands of individual pieces.

But what of the tourist's question? What really happened to the Cherokees? The official Oklahoma view is that they lived happily after statehood, peacefully farming the new acres alloted to them and bettering themselves year by year until they finally became part of white society. But what really took place was one of the most sordid episodes in American history. Barely fifty years ago, the Cherokees and other Indians of the Five Civilized Tribes owned millions of acres, an area as large as many states. Within a generation their holdings had shrunk to a fraction of that, and today they are on the verge of being people without a country.

Since that November morning when the symbolic wedding of Indian and Oklahoma territories was performed, the Cherokees have indeed come a long way. But every step has been downhill.

Angie Debo, a historian who has studied Oklahoma Indians all her life, has written that what followed the allotment of the lands of the Cherokees and other Five Civilized Tribes was "an orgy of plunder and exploitation probably unparalleled in American history." Like other episodes in this country's past, however, the events of this period were to come and go without ever warranting even a sentence in most American history books.

The rest of the United States believed with Senator Henry Dawes that an interest in the Indians' well-being was the only reason their lands had been alloted, but the Cherokees knew better. As early as 1895, one of the delegations in Washington trying to win an exemption from this crippling legislation wrote a bitter letter back home to the Council. "It is seen by the keen eye of speculation," it began, "that if our country is changed as contemplated in the schemes of the Dawes Commission, it will be easy for capitalists and monied men to soon become the owners of millions of acres. But what about our people who are now the legal owners of these lands? The question is easy of answer. Crushed to earth under the hooves of business greed, they will become a homeless throng. No legislation can protect the Indian in his rights. Business has no moral consciousness . . . . It will invoke the aid of a 'higher law' and grasp the Indians' property."

In less time than it took for a boy to grow to manhood, the immense area that had been Indian Territory until 1907 was taken from the Five Civilized Tribes. For decades the Cherokee full bloods had been living self-sufficiently in their Nation, going where they wanted and maintaining their old ways. They were used to picking and choosing from the white man's technology while ignoring the close-fisted notions of property by which he existed. But with allotment, the full blood suddenly found his life totally administered and controlled; and for the first time, his land was a possession. It had been forcibly given to him and would now be just as forcibly taken away.

Most of the white Oklahomans were honest; if they hurt the Indian it was not intentional, but simply because they belonged to a race that saw itself as superior. But there was also ample opportunity for corrupt white men who came to be called "grafters" to fasten themselves like leeches to any Indian with something of value. In a few years, these men had reduced the full bloods from proud independence to abject poverty. The Curtis Act had abolished the sovereign tribal government which had previously shielded the Cherokee full bloods, but it did not offer any substitute protection. Instead the Indian was abandoned to the laws and politics of Oklahoma which were controlled by exactly those people who coveted his land most avidly.

Starting in 1905, the lands were allotted in two parts: a "restricted" homestead of up to 160 acres which could not be sold for 25 years, and a "surplus" of about 40 acres which could be sold. This represented a compromise between the idealists in Washington who were afraid that the Indians' allotments would be quickly eaten up and the local whites who wanted at least a portion of these rich lands for themselves. It was not long before the "surplus" was in the hands of real-estate speculators who relied on the Indians' innocence of the white man's law and his confusion over what "ownership" meant to fleece him of his holdings. One of the speculators' most common techniques was to send agents out into full-blood settlements at the time allotment was going on and induce a wagonload of Indians to come to town. When they arrived, they were persuaded to select their surplus in adjacent sections from rich bottomlands, and to sign deeds in exchange for small sums of money. Then the agents drove them back home again. The Indians had lost land that was technically theirs, although they had never seen it; the speculators had gained, for a few cents an acre, what would become the huge and prosperous white-owned ranches of the future.

But even the protection given the larger "homestead" acreage was half-hearted. Leases were used to get around the restriction against its sale. When a real estate man offered a full blood a fistful of dollars for a lease to his allotment, he often neglected to point out to the Indian the fine-print clause which stated that only a small amount of the money would be paid on signing the papers, and the balance at the end of twenty-five years when a deed to the land could finally be signed. The extended lease was also used to gain control of wide expanses of Indian land, in some cases for as long as ninety-nine years. Such transactions allowed the best of the Five Civilized Tribes' surplus lands to be monopolized by white farmers. As it worked out, few Indians ever got a chance to cultivate their lands and raise their status in life as promised in the schemes of Henry Dawes.

Although unscrupulous, these methods were "legal" as the word was interpreted in the early years of Oklahoma statehood. Fortunes were made overnight in accordance with America's dream of fostering a nation of self-made men. Most grafters, however, did not shrink from more daring ways of acquiring Indian lands. For them, Indian children were an ideal target. Local courts frequently appointed professional guardians for orphans as well as youngsters whose parents were judged "incompetent." This soon became a flourishing business. Once a guardian, the grafter could do whatever he wanted with his wards' lands short of actually selling them. It was not long before guardianships became so lucrative that they were dispensed by local judges as political rewards to people who supported their campaigns for election. Some grafters were appointed guardian for over a hundred Indian children at once. When the uses to which they put this trust became public knowledge, even local whites—who were not noted for sentimentality when it came to Indians—were shocked.

There were countless cases in which valuable minerals were mined from the children's allotments for criminally small sums of money, the guardians getting a kickback from the men they allowed to exploit the lands. Priceless stands of timber were clear-cut overnight. But while the allotments were being scavenged for anything of value, the children often went begging. In one case that became especially notorious, three Indian orphans were found living in the hollow of a tree, drinking from a stream and begging an occasional meal from a neighboring white family while their guardian—who had fifty-one other children under his protection—was collecting large sums from the lease of their lands. He told the court that he spent most of it for the support and education of his wards. If all other means of appropriating the child's property failed, guardians could take advantage of an Oklahoma law that conferred adulthood on a minor who married. People frequently heard of charades in which Indian teenagers were introduced to suitors by their guardians; after a quick courtship and marriage, the youngster would be induced to sign away his allotment. Then he would find that his new spouse had vanished.

The varieties of fraud practiced on Indians were limited only by the grafters' audacity. And the discovery of the fabulously rich Oklahoma oil fields at the turn of the century had only increased their opportunities. The Department of the Interior, officially responsible for protecting Indian land and resources, had more interest in opening up the belly of the earth and letting the black gold jet out into the nation's booming economy. The situation that developed resembled that which took place after the white man's confiscation of Cherokee gold fields seventy years earlier, at a time when the Nation was on the verge of bankruptcy. If the lands had still been held in common, the whole tribe would have profited from the bonanza. Instead a small fraction of the Indians—less than 2 percent—had allotments where oil was discovered. And usually these "oil rich" Indians were induced to squander their wealth or else it was swindled from them by the same techniques that had been used on orphans, since the courts soon decided that they too needed professional guardians.

As Angie Debo writes, "Forgery, embezzlement, criminal conspiracy, and other crimes against Indian property continued with monotonous regularity . . . . It was almost impossible to secure a conviction for outright crime . . . " The grafters did not even stop short of violence to gain control of the lands of the Five Civilized Tribes. In one area, many Choctaw full bloods were induced to make wills bequeathing their property to land dealers. In return, they were to receive a few dollars a month for the rest of their lives. But soon after these agreements were made, an epidemic of mysterious deaths broke out in the Indian settlement. Many people believed that poison had been used. Federal officials threatened an investigation, but nothing came of it.

It was not long before what had been a cohesive society a few years earlier degenerated into chaos. Every aspect of Indian life was affected. After the schools—once the Cherokees' pride—were taken over by the U.S. government at the time of statehood, they changed drastically. When a local politician named John D. Benedict was appointed Commissioner of Schools, he immediately decided that academic training was no longer necessary: Indian boys should learn to work with their hands instead of doing problems in mathematics, and girls should study housekeeping instead of Latin and music. Institutions that once had been the training grounds for Cherokee statesmen changed overnight into little less than prisons.

It was not only that there was no more Cherokee Nation for the graduates of these schools to serve or even that classes were vocational and conducted only in English; worse yet was the fact that the schools were places where the children of an "inferior" race were taught their place. In 1909, when government inspectors from Washington toured these schools, they found them filthy and run down, the children poorly fed and often ill. The desire to learn had vanished and the students were barely literate. (The infamous Bureau of Indian Affairs boarding schools have their origins in this era. As late as 1969, a team of federal investigators found that most students at the BIA school at Chilocco, Oklahoma, were poorly nourished and undereducated, and that some of them—the "discipline problems"—were kept handcuffed in the basement for up to eighteen hours and occasionally were beaten badly.)

At the time of the allotment of its lands, the Cherokee Nation comprised over 4,500,000 acres; by 1930 only about one-tenth of this area was still in Indian hands. The original intent of the legislation—transforming Indians into successful small farmers—was a disastrous failure; fewer Cherokees worked farms than had done so at the time of statehood. The full blood had been pushed deep into the hill country that is his home today, leaving the productive areas in white hands. He supported himself by cutting wood, hunting small game, and cultivating small gardens.

When a Congressional committee investigating Indian affairs came through northeastern Oklahoma in 1930, a young Cherokee full blood told them: "We have not very much land now. If we keep on selling it piece by piece, after a while the Indians will not have any land in this country, not one piece left. Now, what are we going to do? Are we going to be turned out like hogs or something like that?"

At the time of Oklahoma statehood, when Redbird Smith and the other full bloods turned their backs on the new white government that had been forced on them and withdrew to the hills of the Ozarks, it seemed as if the history of The Real People had come to a standstill. The new state developed rapidly into one of the richest of the United States, and the Cherokee full blood quietly led his life behind the "green curtain" that shielded him from the white man's view. His unobtrusiveness allowed him to survive, but it also abetted the white myths which said that the Cherokee had long since given up his native ways and become part of the mainstream of Oklahoma life. Even if someone had been available to chronicle the life of the Cherokee full bloods from 1906 until the early 1960s, there probably would not have been much to record in the uneventful life of these hill communities. It was as if the people had folded themselves into a cocoon.

In the mid-1960s, a young American anthropologist named Albert Wahrhaftig spent a year traveling through the area and taking the first census of the Cherokees that had been made in decades. He found that far from dying out, there were over ten thousand full bloods in more than fifty growing backwoods communities where they had fled at the direction of Redbird Smith and the other Nighthawks. These people dressed and acted like their rural white neighbors, but Wahrhaftig found that they were strongly traditional in outlook and folkways. They maintained the rituals around the log Baptist churches as they had at the turn of the century; they still held dances at certain festive times of the year; and more than half of them spoke only Cherokee.

But these full bloods are still in the downward spiral that began when the state of Oklahoma grasped them to its bosom over fifty years ago. Today the average per family income is less than two thousand dollars a year, about one-half the average of poor white families in the area; and usually a majority of the people in these communities are unemployed. Women take whatever work they can find, usually as "baby sitters" for their white neighbors, which means they do hard housework for a few dollars a day. Their husbands make only a little more than this when they are fortunate enough to get seasonal work in the nurseries or chicken-processing plants in the area. Surveys made in the mid-1960s show that while a few of these Cherokees had managed to keep enough land to do small farming up to the early 1950s, hardly any still own land today. For the most part the monthly check of the social worker is replacing farm income or the low wages of the rural white employer as the Cherokees' staff of life. While they comprise only 13 percent of the population in the northeastern part of what was once their Nation, these full bloods make up more than 35 percent of those on welfare. Better than half the families need old-age assistance, aid to dependent children, or some other kind of government help even to subsist.

Since Oklahomans have yet to admit officially what the grafters did to the Indians, they cannot understand why these people are poor. They say it is because the Cherokees "lack initiative," but in truth it is because they are imprisoned in a caste system that keeps them on the bottom of the social ladder while insisting that they stay there by their own choice. It is a system that is all-encompassing. Children from these full-blood communities now go to rural public schools run by white people mainly for the benefit of their own children. By an early age they have suffered enough humiliation to kill their educational promise. They are told to compete for learning and grades even though the life of their people is based on cooperation; they are seen not as culturally different, but as socially inferior.

In the hearings held before Senator Robert Kennedy's Subcommittee on Indian Education in 1968, one Cherokee parent said simply, "Some teachers are unable to love the Cherokee Indian. I wish they could love the Cherokee and the white the same. They should." These parents sense the futility of a system in which, even if their children manage to graduate, there is little for them to do. They can only cut themselves off from their community, go to cities like Tulsa to look for work, and run the risk of winding up in the ghetto at the bottom of the urban heap. Thus Cherokee children tend to leave school early. Cherokees average about five years of education, three years less than their poor white neighbors and five years less than the average in the rest of the state.

In school and out, the Cherokee today can succeed only by giving up the ways of his people. Andrew Dreadfulwater, a full-blood leader, describes this conflict: "There are two kinds of Cherokee. One that thinks they are white people and think they are not Cherokees. The other, of course, knows he is a Cherokee and acts that way. The Cherokee who knows he is Cherokee and tries to help his people, immediately he is stopped and loses his job. The other kind is not concerned with Cherokee problems, ignores them and does not lose his job."

But schools and the subtle pressure exerted on full bloods to make them forsake the ways of their people and become like whites are only part of the problem. There is also the question of the land, the small remnant of Cherokee lands that daily sift like sand through the Indians' fingers.

There are isolated cases where whites fence in Cherokee lands next to theirs and are able to keep them because the Indian is too poor to pay the surveyor to testify for him in court. But for the most part, the full blood's enemy today is not the grafter of the past, but the law itself. For instance, even though over half of the full bloods need some form of government aid to survive, when they apply for it they immediately collide with a state ruling that no one owning more than forty acres of land is eligible for welfare or old-age assistance. This does not affect the young Cherokees who were born landless and who share a few acres with parents or other relatives. But aging Indians who have managed to hold on to their 160-acre allotments must now sell most of these lands and spend the money before becoming eligible for the public assistance funds that keep them from starving.

At the time of Redbird Smith the Cherokees retreated to steep and hilly areas they thought no one would ever want. But even this area has become valuable now that the state of Oklahoma has decided to develop its mountain regions to attract tourists. The U.S. Army Corps of Engineers bulldozes more of the full bloods' remaining allotments every year to build the campgrounds and man-made lakes that will turn the area into a "sportsman's paradise." The Bureau of Indian Affairs, which is supposed to protect the Indians' resources, not only lets this happen, but has itself contributed to the loss of lands through carelessness or outright connivance with the local power structure. For example, the BIA constantly encourages full bloods to trade their acres in the hills for small lots closer to town where they have a better chance of finding employment. And when a

Cherokee dies and leaves several heirs, the Bureau routinely sells the allotment and distributes the proceeds instead of trying to work out a solution that will keep the land in one piece and in the hands of the Indian family.

What does all this add up to? By the government's own estimate, the remaining full-blood land is going into white hands at the rate of five thousand acres a year. As a Cherokee full blood named George Groundhog says, "Nobody, not the BIA or anyone else, is doing anything about this. One of these days we're going to wake up and there won't be any land left. That is the day when there won't be any Indians left either. Maybe that's what they want."

The land is the key to the Indians' future, and the vast majority of Cherokee full bloods agree that its slow but steady disappearance overshadows all their other problems. Without the precious acres still left to them, they will become displaced persons in the white world; a people whose own heritage is no longer a living option, and who can find no comfort in being replicas of their white neighbors.

Still, the vulnerability of their lands is only the worst of many problems the Cherokees face. They must also cope with other kinds of humiliation and sharp dealing from the whites with whom they come in contact. Playing on the popular notion that all Indians are "stupid," many rural merchants sell goods at two prices—a regular price and a higher, "Indian price." Many whites think that all Indians are alcoholics, a racial stereotype that occasionally can have tragic consequences. When Senator Robert Kennedy visited Tahlequah in 1968, he was told about a seventy-six-year-old Cherokee man who had recently become ill while walking home from the grocery store. He had fallen to the ground, and when the city police arrived, they automatically assumed that any Indian lying on the sidewalk in broad daylight

135

must be drunk. The old man was taken to jail where he stayed for several hours; his family was not allowed to see him. After several hours the police realized that he was sick, and took him to the hospital. But it was too late. He died that night.

Even the Cherokees' small welfare checks are often the target of petty swindles by whites. When a fire in a small town not far from Tahlequah destroyed the general store and the post office branch located inside it, there was a crisis in the local economy. The store owner, who had been in the habit of giving the local full bloods high-priced credit toward the end of each month, counted as much as they did on the arrival of the welfare checks. After the fire, he persuaded the postmaster to give the checks directly to him as soon as they arrived; then he went through the community trying to force the Indians to endorse their checks over to him. When some of them complained that this was illegal and that the postmaster should never have given out mail addressed to them, the store owner got the local sheriff to drive him to the Cherokees' homes in his car and lend the weight of his office to the collection efforts.

Armin Saeger, a white social worker who was formerly with the U.S. Public Health Service in Tahlequah, recounts a similar instance involving a Cherokee widow who depended on welfare payments to help feed her eight children. A merchant in the small Oklahoma town where she lived decided to gain control of her monthly check and went to court to have himself appointed the woman's legal guardian. "His contention that the woman was incompetent," Saeger says, "was supported by the welfare worker and the judge, who made a ruling without even meeting her or holding a formal hearing. The first thing the woman knew, her check was going to the merchant, who doles out small amounts to her every month and probably never accounts for the rest."

The full bloods accept all this because they have no choice. Often they may be seen sitting on the porches of their cabins talking in the soft, throaty tones of their language and telling the stories many Cherokees know by heart. One is about a snake that started out no bigger than a man's finger and kept growing bigger and bigger, eating everything in sight until there was nothing large enough left to satisfy his appetite. "That snake," so the tale ends, "is just like the white man."

While the Cherokees' miseries multiply, they have seen the rise of a new tribal government that rules in their name and spends money belonging to them on projects they often know nothing about. For the full bloods, the situation they face is symbolized by W. W. Keeler, the man who governs as their Principal Chief, but who is only one-sixteenth Indian and neither speaks the Cherokee language nor participates in their way of life. He is the descendant of whites who came into the Territory not long before statehood, marrying into the tribe and then going into the land and oil businesses. He lives on a mammoth ranch and heads Phillips Petroleum, one of the giant Oklahoma oil corporations built on a foundation of Indian wealth.

When Keeler was first made Principal Chief by President Harry S Truman in 1949, there was no outcry. Since the tribal government had been abolished chiefs had occasionally been appointed when a paper had to be signed in connection with the allotment of lands. (The fact that the President made the appointment was a vestige of the Cherokees' former importance.) Everyone understood Keeler had gotten the position less because of his fraction of Indian blood than because he was a rising executive with the most influential corporation in Oklahoma. The position carried with it no power or authority because there was nobody to govern and nothing to govern with. Although Keeler formed a tribal government, the chieftainship was ceremonial, like being a member of a fraternal lodge, and the Cherokees didn't take it seriously.

But in 1961, this changed. The U.S. Indian Claims Court, established in 1946 to compensate tribes for lands the government had taken over the centuries, awarded the Cherokees a $15 million settlement for the Cherokee Outlet, which the tribe had been forced to sell in 1893 at a price far below fair market value. After attorneys' fees were deducted, the money was divided up among the more than forty thousand people —a large majority whites with little if any Indian blood— who were either on the roll made at the time of allotment or descendants of those who were. Each person received a payment of $280. But afterward, there was still some $2 million left over in fractional or unclaimed shares. This went to W. W. Keeler's tribal government, which had now taken to calling itself "The Cherokee Nation." These dollars were to be the building blocks for his private vision of how the Cherokees should face the modern world.

Keeler's first concern was for the past. Obtaining matching grants from state and federal governments, he appropriated $100,000 of the Indians' money for the construction of the Cultural Center which few of the Cherokees knew about and even fewer wanted. As work on the re-created village and the amphitheater was begun, a large, modern tribal headquarters was being built on the outskirts of Tahlequah. One corner of this building is devoted to a crafts shop selling hand-made Indian items like ten-dollar bead necklaces which take the Cherokee a day to make and for which he is paid three dollars each; another part is rented out to the local

Bureau of Indian Affairs agency which works along with Keeler's government to administer the full bloods.

The future of the Cherokees was also looked after. There was to be economic development for the Indians, although the full bloods were not to be given an opportunity to indicate *their* priorities for spending the leftover claims money in the tribal treasury. By 1967 Keeler had decided that Cherokee money should be loaned out to small companies making such products as heating equipment and fiberglass boats. It was thought that the loans would induce these firms to open factories in Cherokee country and give work to the chronically unemployed Indians, thus getting them off welfare. But things didn't work according to the plan. Even though more than $200,000 was loaned out, less than 50 Cherokees were ever hired, fewer than the number of whites employed by the companies.

Today, Keeler's tribal government boasts about the fact that it has arranged for eighty-three Cherokees to be employed by Western Electric Company doing electronic assemblies (and thus playing on the pervasive notion that Indians are qualified primarily for jobs requiring manual dexterity), but it does not mention that only half of these jobs are full time or that only twenty-five of the employees are men; the favoring of women further damages the ecology of the Indian family. Much also is made of the fact that Phillips Products, a subsidiary of Phillips Petroleum that makes plastic pipe, now has a plant in the small northeastern Oklahoma town of Pryor, where two-thirds of the employees are Cherokee. Forty of the plant's sixty employees are indeed Indians, but for reasons that are not entirely altruistic.

The plant manager, O. E. Larsen, says, "We hire Indians here because of Mr. Keeler's interest in them, but also because it makes good economic sense." The Cherokees are employed through the Bureau of Indian Affairs' employment assistance program in which Indians hired to "learn a trade" have up to one-half of their wages paid by the government for as many as eighteen months.

None of the Cherokees at the Pryor plant are supervisors and much of their value comes from the fact that they are a passive, inexpensive labor force. "Your minority people," Larsen says, "they aren't so transient. There are a lot of Indians living in this area with their families and all, and you know they aren't just going to up and leave here. I mean if you train up a group of them, they aren't likely to go running off to a place like Chicago hunting a better-paying job with the skills you've given them. We hire a lot of Indians here because we have the kind of low-paying jobs they qualify for because of their lack of education. Now if we had a lot of jobs paying four dollars or so an hour, you'd see our ratio of Indians to white workers flop right on over."

Keeler's version of the Cherokee Nation continues to promote its plans regardless of their failure and regardless of the fact that the people have shown little enthusiasm for them. (It was not until 1971, after already governing for some twenty years and spending much of the Indians' money on projects like the Cultural Center and the various "economic development" programs, that Chief Keeler—perhaps reacting to adverse publicity in books, magazine articles, and newspaper stories—finally held tribal elections. Ballots were sent to all those on the tribal roll that had been made in the days of allotment—the mixed bloods and whites far outnumbering the full bloods—and he won.) These plans conceive of the Cherokees as clock-punching laborers, cogs in the wheels of industry, derelicts to be gotten off welfare, or some other abstraction from the white man's brain. It may even mean well, but Keeler's tribal government prohibits the full blood from developing in accordance with his own priorities and in ways that will vitalize, not weaken, the remaining Cherokee communities.

Mildred Ballenger, a seventy-year-old Tahlequah woman whose grandmother came over the Trail of Tears and who has been involved with Cherokee affairs a good part of her life, is one of many who would like to see Chief Keeler's power broken. But sometimes it appears impossible. "If things don't seem to look too bad down here," she says, "it's only because you can't see them. Underneath all the sweet talk about development and industry and all that, the Cherokees are getting smothered—by local power, by Oklahoma politics, and by big business." W. W. Keeler has used his position with Phillips Petroleum not only to gain the chieftainship of his version of the Cherokee Nation, but also to attain power within the Bureau of Indian Affairs and the Department of the Interior. White officials listen, but Indians all over the country see him only as a symbol of the problems they face in taking hold once again of their own destiny.

While W. W. Keeler sits in the boardroom of his oil company, speaking for a people he doesn't know or understand, the problems facing the Indians fester and grow worse. The full bloods have tried to do something about them and might succeed if they were ever able to command the resources which have instead gone to satisfy the whims of those they derisively call "white Indians." But even so, they have made it clear that they are not going to sit by while their culture is threatened once more with extinction.

The first sign that the Cherokees knew the stakes they face came in the spring of 1966 when John Chewie, a full blood living near the small Oklahoma town of Jay, was

arrested for going into the woods and killing a deer out of
season and without a license. The round-faced, raven-haired
Chewie was known around town; he had had run-ins with
the law on other occasions. Occasionally he worked part-time
for local whites, but mostly he was unemployed. He killed
the deer for food, not for what the white man calls sport.

At another time perhaps Chewie would have received
the usual justice meted out to Cherokees: a patronizing rep-
rimand and a few days in jail to teach a "lesson." But on the
day he came to trial, the usually shy Cherokee full bloods of
this area began to filter into town, climbing down from
pick-up trucks and standing in groups around the Jay court-
house. They were armed with the shotguns and rifles they,
too, used to hunt game out of season and without licenses to
make sure that there was occasionally meat on the family
table. The men stood there in silent vigil, not threatening
anyone but still sending shivers of fear through the town.
When it became clear that John Chewie would not be con-
victed, they went home as quietly as they had come.

This spontaneous demonstration did not mean that
Cherokees had changed their traditionally mild ways and
were going to walk through the countryside armed and
shouting Red Power slogans, although there were those in
Oklahoma who feared such an outbreak. This protest was
part of a larger movement brought on by the fact that the
Cherokees once again felt that a time had come when their
culture was in danger of disappearing.

After the Nation was abolished, Cherokee became almost
exclusively a spoken language. Only a handful of medicine
men-conjurers and ministers of the Cherokee Baptist Church
still read it. But at about the time that John Chewie went to
trial, a renaissance among the full bloods was beginning.
The Five County Cherokee Movement (so called because

most Cherokees are concentrated in five northeastern Oklahoma counties) was formed in 1966. It began as a secret organization reminiscent of the Keetowah Society at the time of the Civil War and Redbird Smith's Nighthawks. In a Declaration, the Five County Cherokees said: "We meet in a time of darkness to seek the path to the light. We come together, just as our fathers have always done, to do these things. . . . We offer ourselves as the voice of the Cherokee people. For many years our people have not spoken and have not been heard. Now we gather as brothers and sisters."

With the help of a few white university researchers who were willing to come to the Tahlequah area and brave the anger of local whites, the Cherokees set up a newspaper, began to print Cherokee literature again, and even started a local radio program. Their language came into use, and their genius for organization—dormant for many years— was revived once more. The full bloods thought back to the days when they had controlled the destiny of the tribe, speaking through great leaders like John Ross. Soon meetings were being held in the Cherokee Baptist Churches. Full bloods began to talk of themselves as "Keetowahs," as they had during the Civil War, allotment, and other critical moments in their past. By 1967, the spontaneous outrage that had led to the formation of the Five County Cherokee movement had swept through all the full-blood settlements, and the Original Cherokee Community Organization was organized to resist W. W. Keeler and the white world generally.

The OCCO, as it is called, rents a small three-room storefront on a quiet Tahlequah side street. It has no money to loan to white businesses; there are no secretaries or receptionists as at Keeler's elaborate tribal headquarters. There is just a staff of three full bloods elected by the communities and a mimeograph machine that grinds out a monthly newsletter with alternating columns of Cherokee and English. The OCCO hasn't done anything the white world would consider dramatic. Local judges have routinely dismissed most of the suits filed by its volunteer attorneys to keep the land from disappearing or the welfare checks from being swindled. Yet the organization is there, informing the full bloods of what is being done to them, cutting wood for aged Indians, holding weekly meetings in outlying districts to weld the people together, and doing whatever else it can to stop the forces arrayed against the Cherokees. Led by full bloods with names like Dreadfulwater and Fourkiller, the OCCO has functioned as a government-in-exile. It has kept W. W. Keeler's organization from functioning completely as a law unto itself, and has been a rallying point for the Cherokees' concerns about their future.

There is nothing permanent about this organization; it is only the most recent of several attempts by the full bloods to preserve their heritage. But if the OCCO disappears tomorrow, as it may, something else will spring up to take its place. For the Cherokees know now that they have finally run out of time and space, and they fear that the white man will penetrate their settlements, take the last of their land, and convince their children to go live like him in his doomed cities. They know that this is perilously close and if it happens, they will be the last of their people to walk the earth.

EPILOGUE

A few miles outside Tahlequah there is a cleared-off place in a large field. The Cherokees call it the Redbird Smith Stompgrounds, named after the leader who brought the full bloods together fifty years ago and whose sons and grandsons still live in this area. I stopped there once in late spring. The grounds were empty, the semicircle of old wooden platforms totally deserted, charred logs sitting in the open fireplace. There had been people there recently, but it seemed as though there was no one within miles and that no one would come again. But I knew that by midsummer Cherokees from settlements all over the area would gather here for a weekend arriving in old cars and pick-up trucks and bringing tents and bedrolls. The platforms would be filled with people greeting old friends, laughing and talking; a large fire would be built and the smell of frying food would fill the air. There would be music and chants, and some of the women would strap old-style shakers made of terrapin shells on their legs or perhaps just tin cans filled with pebbles. Then they would do the stomp dances and sing the songs that connect them to older times.

There is something defective in the white culture that has not only taken almost everything these people once possessed, but also seeks to destroy finally the world mirrored in this dance. Is it just obsessive greed? Or is it the dangerous jealousy of people who suspect that their way of relating to their fellow men is drastically limited in comparison with the Indians'—that they have lived only for themselves so long that they are now, in the words of a current Indian leader named Earl Old Person, a series of "one-man reservations"? It is hard to tell. But understanding why the white man has pursued the Cherokees so relentlessly over the centuries is now less important than making sure they are allowed to keep the little they have left. This much they have earned.

BIBLIOGRAPHICAL
NOTE

This book attempts to record the long ordeal of the Cherokees from pre-colonial times to the present, but there are many valuable works about episodes in their tragic history. Some of the best are the earliest, written by travelers and adventurers who were the first whites to come in contact with the Cherokees. Lt. Henry Timberlake visited the tribe in the mid-1700s and published his observations in *Memoirs* (London, 1765). James Adair, the sometime Indian agent who became acquainted with the Cherokees at about the same time, wrote about them in his *History of the American Indian* (London, 1775.) Despite his odd conviction that the Cherokees were actually one of the lost tribes of Israel, Adair's book contains vital first-hand information, as does botanist William Bartram's *Travels* (London, 1792).

In the 1880s, anthropologist James Mooney spent years talking with old people in the tribe and patiently wrote down what they told him. He was able to collect the legends and folklore of The Real People, knowledge that otherwise would have been forgotten. This material, which gives the most vivid sense of the Cherokee world view, appears in Mooney's "Sacred Formulas of the Cherokees" (Bureau of American Ethnology, 7th Annual Report, 1888), and "Myths of the Cherokees" (Bureau of American Ethnology, 19th Annual Report, 1900).

The standard history of the tribe is Grace Steele Woodward's *The Cherokees* (Norman, Oklahoma, 1963). Although less readable than Marion Starkey's *The Cherokee Nation* (New York, 1946), it contains the most complete record of the tribe from earliest times until the brutal aftermath of the Civil War. Yet Woodward's book is marred by a tone of cultural superiority that has no place in a work about this admirable people. Her opening sentence reads: "The emergence of any primitive Indian tribe or nation from dark savagery into the sun of civilization is a significant event." Given the long continuity that connects America's genocidal wars against Indian tribes with its wars in Indochina, it is clear that historians should be wary of easy generalizations about "civilization" and "savagery."

John Brown's *Old Frontiers* (Kingsport, Tennessee, 1938) traces the history of the Cherokees from the colonial period to removal, with special attention given to Dragging Canoe and his Chickamaugans. In *Tecumseh: Vision of Glory* (Indianapolis, 1956), Glenn Tucker describes the attempts of this powerful statesman to form an Indian confederacy to halt the white man's inexorable advance across the frontier. Grant Foreman's *Sequoyah* (Norman, Oklahoma, 1938) tells the little that is known about this remarkable man and the events leading to his invention of the Cherokee alphabet. *Cherokee Messenger* (Norman, Oklahoma,

1936) by Althea Bass recounts the life of Samuel Austin Worcester, and Rachel Eaton's *John Ross and the Cherokee Indians* (Chicago, 1921), although sketchy and incomplete, is the only biography of the Principal Chief.

A recent book, Thurman Wilkins' *Cherokee Tragedy* (New York, 1970) is an excellent study of the expulsion of the Cherokees from their eastern homeland and is built around sympathetic sketches of Major Ridge, his son John, and Elias Boudinot. Wilkins argues that members of the Treaty Party acted out of the highest patriotism, not from the selfish motives ascribed to them by most historians.

The immediate events leading up to the Trail of Tears are dramatically recreated in Dale Van Every's *The Disinherited* (New York, 1966), while the removal of all the Five Civilized Tribes is the subject of Grant Foreman's *Indian Removal* (Norman, 1932). In his *Political History of the Cherokee Nation, 1838–1907* (Norman, 1938), Morris J. Wardell describes the Cherokees' attempt to reestablish their government in Indian Territory, the diastrous consequences of the American Civil War, and the advent of Oklahoma statehood. The fight against allotment, and the graft and corruption which followed statehood are the subjects of Angie Debo's major study, *And Still the Waters Run* (Princeton, 1940). Emmett Starr mentions the Redbird Smith movement in his *History of the Cherokee Indians and Their Legends* (Oklahoma City, 1921). Stan Steiner's *The New Indians* (New York, 1968) has a valuable chapter on the John Chewie affair and the reawakening of a nationalistic spirit among Cherokees today.

And finally, the crucially important work of Albert Wahrhaftig and Robert K. Thomas of the University of Chicago in "discovering" contemporary Cherokee full bloods, as well as the formation of the Original Cherokee Community Organization, are covered at length in volume 5, part 2 of the 1968 report of the U.S. Senate Subcommittee on Indian Education chaired by Senator Robert Kennedy (U.S. Government Printing Office).

AUTHOR'S NOTE

This book was written primarily for young people, but I hope that adults, too, will find it readable and worthwhile. The story of the Cherokees needs to be told over and again. Indians have always tended to become "relevant" whenever American society is undergoing a moral crisis such as that brought on by the war in Vietnam. But when the fever passes, Indians sink back into the obscurity which for them has been the status quo. It has happened before; unfortunately, it seems to be happening again. The eminent American jurist Felix Cohen once commented that this nation's treatment of the Indian is a miner's canary for our democracy: it indicates the amount of poison in the political air at any given time.

The struggle of the Cherokees and other tribes continues whether or not periodic episodes of cultural guilt bring their plight to the public consciousness. I would like to thank some of the people in Tahlequah, Oklahoma, who have kept the faith for a long time and who spent time talking to me when I was there: Armin Saeger, Stuart Trapp, members of the Original Cherokee Community Center, and most of all Mr. and Mrs. T. L. Ballenger. I also benefited from the experiences of Al Wahrhaftig who did activist field work with the Cherokees in the early 1960s under trying conditions often imposed by local whites.

I want to thank my editor Shirley Dolgoff at Holt. I also want to remember Maryjo Collier, with whom I picked wild-flowers in the Oklahoma Ozarks; and Doris Collier, who, along with Corinne Clark, was always anxious to know when this book would be published. And I hope my children Andrew and Caitlin will enjoy reading it someday.

PETER COLLIER
Oakland, California
March, 1973

LEADING FIGURES
IN CHEROKEE
HISTORY

ATTAKULLACULLA

("Little Carpenter"). Cherokee chief during mid-1700s,
known for his skill as a diplomat.

BLOODY FELLOW

Chickamaugan warrior (see
Dragging Canoe).

ELIAS BOUDINOT

(Original name: Buck Watie).
First editor of the *Cherokee
Phoenix*; sponsor of the Treaty
of New Echota; executed in
1839.

ELIAS CORNELIUS BOUDINOT

(Son of Elias Boudinot). Urged
Cherokee support of the South
during the Civil War; afterward was a railroad lobbyist,
and later promoted white settlement of Indian Territory.

153

HENRY DAWES — U.S. Senator from Massachusetts (1875–1893), sponsor of the Dawes Act (1887) which forced individual ownership of tribal lands on Indians.

DOUBLEHEAD — Chickamaugan (see Dragging Canoe); executed by The Ridge in 1807 for selling tribal lands illegally.

DRAGGING CANOE — (Son of Attakullaculla). From 1775 to his death in 1792, leader of the Chickamaugans, those Cherokees who warred against whites during this period.

ANDREW JACKSON — Seventh President of the United States (1829-1837); leading proponent of removal of all eastern Indians to Indian Territory.

THOMAS JEFFERSON — Third President of the United States (1801-1809); signed the Georgia Compact, which led to expulsion of the Cherokees from their eastern homeland.

WILLIAM W. KEELER — Oklahoma oil man. Appointed Principal Chief of the Cherokees in 1949, a position he still holds.

OLD TASSEL — Prominent peace chief during 1770s and 1780s when the Chickamaugans were fighting white settlers.

THE RIDGE	(Named "He Who Walks on Mountain Top" at birth, later called The Ridge and, finally, Major Ridge). At first a warrior, then, in the early 1800s, a noted Cherokee statesman and advocate of white culture; later a sponsor of the Treaty of New Echota; executed in 1839.
JOHN RIDGE	(Son of Major Ridge, cousin of Elias Boudinot). At first fought against removal, later supported Treaty of New Echota; executed in 1839.
JOHN ROSS	Principal Chief of the Cherokee Nation from 1827 until his death in 1866; leader of the tribe during its worst crises and greatest achievements.
WILLIAM P. ROSS	(Nephew of John Ross). Editor of *The Cherokee Advocate*; Principal Chief of the Cherokees (1866-1867, 1872-1874).
SEQUOYAH	(English name: George Guess or Gist). Completed creation of the Cherokee alphabet in 1821.
REDBIRD SMITH	In early 1900s, leader of the revived Keetowah Society which opposed individual allotment of Cherokee tribal lands.

TSALI	Legendary Cherokee martyr who sacrificed his life in 1838 to save those Cherokees who had fled from United States soldiers enforcing removal.
BUCK WATIE	(see Elias Boudinot)
STAND WATIE	Brother of Elias Boudinot and cousin of John Ridge; Treaty Party leader after 1839; Confederate General during the Civil War.
SAMUEL AUSTIN WORCESTER	(Also called The Messenger). White missionary who lived with the Cherokees from 1825 until his death in 1852; worked closely with Elias Boudinot on the *Cherokee Phoenix*; defendant in *Samuel A. Worcester* v. *The State of Georgia*, 1832.

IMPORTANT
DATES

1540   Cherokees see whites for the first time when DeSoto's explorers enter their territory.

1673   First contact is made between Cherokees and English colonists when explorers from the Virginia colony arrive in Cherokee country.

1711   Cherokees fight the Tuscarora Indians; when Cherokees realize that both they and the Tuscaroras have been deceived by Virginia colonists, Cherokees war against whites.

1738   A smallpox epidemic causes the death of half the Cherokee Nation.

1775   Cherokees make first major land cession to whites: what is today Kentucky and middle Tennessee is sold to The Transylvania Land Company for two thousand pounds and a log cabin filled with trading goods.

1785 Cherokees sign the Treaty of Hopewell, their first treaty with the United States government.

1791 Cherokees sign the Treaty of Holston with the United States government, which obtains the exclusive right to trade with the Cherokees and promises to help the tribe attain "a greater degree of civilization" by furnishing it with farm implements and technical advice.

1801 First Moravian missionary school is established in Cherokee country.

1802 President Thomas Jefferson signs the Georgia Compact, which provides that the United States government will acquire all western lands claimed by the State of Georgia in return for the promise to extinguish all Indian title to lands within this state's borders.

1807 Doublehead is executed by The Ridge for selling Cherokee lands.

1808 The first group of Cherokees (later known as Old Settlers) voluntarily emigrate to Arkansas to avoid adopting white culture. In 1828 they are forced to move across the Mississippi into Indian Territory. By 1838 there are four thousand Old Settlers in Indian Territory.

1813- Under the leadership of Andrew Jackson, Cherokees fight
1814 in United States war against the Creek "Red Sticks."

1821 Sequoyah perfects a Cherokee alphabet which soon leads to almost total literacy in the Cherokee Nation.

1822 The Cherokees establish a Supreme Court.

1827 The first written constitution of the Cherokee Nation is adopted; John Ross is elected Principal Chief.

1828 The Cherokee Nation's first newspaper, the *Cherokee Phoenix*, begins publication. Andrew Jackson is elected

President of the United States. Gold is discovered on Cherokee lands in Georgia.

1830   The Indian Removal Bill is passed by Congress; it provides for the final removal of southeastern Indian tribes across the Mississippi to Indian Territory. Indian Codes are passed by the State of Georgia.

1832   *Samuel A. Worcester* v. *The State of Georgia.* A landmark decision by the U.S. Supreme Court decrees that "The Cherokee Nation is a distinct community, occupying its own territory . . . in which the laws of Georgia can have no right to enter. . . ." President Jackson refuses to enforce this decision. Georgia holds a public lottery for Cherokee lands.

1835   The Treaty of New Echota, providing for the removal of the Cherokee Nation to Indian Territory, is secretly signed by a few Cherokee leaders (the Treaty Party); this treaty is ratified in the United States Senate by one vote.

1838   The Trail of Tears. The Cherokees are forced to march from their eastern homeland to Indian Territory. Of the eighteen thousand Cherokees who begin, four thousand die along the way.

1839   Major Ridge, John Ridge and Elias Boudinot are executed for signing the Treaty of New Echota.

1851   The Cherokee Nation establishes Male and Female Seminaries to provide its young people with higher education.

1861   Civil War begins. The Cherokee Nation is forced to ally itself with the Confederate government. In Indian Territory the Civil War is paralleled in civil strife between full bloods (the Keetowah Society) and mixed bloods (the Knights of the Golden Circle).

1866   In a post-war treaty between the Cherokees and the

United States government, the Cherokees lose their western lands and provisions are made for United States courts to take jurisdiction in Indian Territory, for the American military to erect posts there and for railroads to extend their lines into the Territory. Death of John Ross.

1871　The first railroad enters Cherokee lands.

1887　The Dawes Act is passed; it requires private, individual ownership of land traditionally held in common by each American Indian tribe.

1889　"Unassigned lands" in Indian Territory are opened to settlement by whites known as "Boomers."

1890　Oklahoma Territory is organized out of the western half of Indian Territory. The two territories coexist for the next decade.

1893　The Cherokee Outlet is opened to white settlement. The Dawes Commission arrives in Indian Territory to negotiate for the allotment of all Indian lands.

1898　The Curtis Act is passed. It abolishes Cherokee tribal courts and laws, makes the actions of the Council subject to the approval of the federal government, and forces allotment on the Indians.

1900-
1905　An official roll of the Cherokees is made in preparation for the division of tribal lands. Redbird Smith organizes opposition to allotment among Cherokee full bloods. In 1905 allotment begins.

1906　The government of the Cherokee Nation is dissolved by the United States Congress.

1907　Oklahoma Territory and Indian Territory are joined together in the new state of Oklahoma.

1914　William Rogers, the last elected chief of the Cherokees, resigns.

1949   W. W. Keeler, a Bartlesville, Oklahoma, oilman, is appointed Principal Chief of the Cherokees by President Truman.

1961   The Cherokees are awarded $15 million by the United States Claims Commission in payment for the Cherokee Outlet. Chief Keeler gets jurisdiction over $2 million of this amount.

1963   The University of Chicago cross-cultural study project "discovers" full-blood Cherokee communities in northeastern Oklahoma hills.

1966   John Chewie's arrest for killing a deer out of season provokes the organization of the Five Counties Cherokees, out of which grows the Original Cherokee Community Organization.

INDEX

ABOUT THE AUTHOR

PETER COLLIER is a writer whose work has been published in many periodicals, including *The New York Times, Ramparts,* the *Sunday London Times* and *Saturday Review.* He became interested in the Cherokees as a result of a general interest in Indian affairs and has visited many reservations and other Indian communities, including Cherokee settlements in Oklahoma. He is the author of numerous articles about contemporary Indian life. Mr. Collier, his wife and their two children live in Oakland, California.